LIFE AND
BUSINESS
LESSONS

GET
SMARTER

SEYMOUR SCHULICH

with Derek DeCloet

LIFE AND
BUSINESS
LESSONS

GET SMARTER

KEY PORTER BOOKS

Library and Archives Canada Cataloguing in Publication

Schulich, Seymour
    Get smarter: life and business lessons / Seymour Schulich; with Derek DeCloet.

Includes index.
ISBN 978-1-55263-942-9 (bound).—ISBN 978-1-55470-115-5 (pbk.)

1. Entrepreneurship. 2. Success in business. 3. Conduct of life. 4. Young adults—Conduct of life. I. Title.

HF5386.S33 2007   650.1   C2007-901832-7

ONTARIO ARTS COUNCIL
CONSEIL DES ARTS DE L'ONTARIO

THE CANADA COUNCIL | LE CONSEIL DES ARTS
FOR THE ARTS | DU CANADA
SINCE 1957 | DEPUIS 1957

The publisher gratefully acknowledges the support of the Canada Council for the Arts and the Ontario Arts Council for its publishing program. We acknowledge the support of the Government of Ontario through the Ontario Media Development Corporation's Ontario Book Initiative.

We acknowledge the financial support of the Government of Canada through the Book Publishing Industry Development Program (BPIDP) for our publishing activities.

Cartoons copyright ©2007 by Ted Goff

Key Porter Books Limited
Six Adelaide Street East, Tenth Floor
Toronto, Ontario
Canada M5C 1H6
www.keyporter.com

Cover design: Roberto de Vicq de Cumptich
Text design: Martin Gould
Electronic formatting: Jean Lightfoot Peters

Printed and bound in Canada

08 09 10 11 12 5 4 3 2 1

For my father, Julius (1898–1985), who supplied
a lot of the wisdom contained herein

TABLE OF CONTENTS

LIFE AND
BUSINESS
LESSONS

GET
SMARTER

INTRODUCTION

This book is an effort to deliver to a twenty- to forty-year-old person the life lessons learned by a sixty-seven-year-old Canadian billionaire. The word "billionaire" is a very crude and inaccurate measure of how well I have played the game of life. I hope it creates enough curiosity to motivate readers in this age group to get away from their cell phones, BlackBerrys, emails, and computers long enough to acquire some knowledge the old-fashioned way: through reading a book.

I grew up in a time of no computers, television, or jet planes. At eight years of age, I went to the closest public library and made a wonderful discovery: I could borrow three books for three weeks. I started reading a book a week. If you read a page a minute, then set aside an hour a day, it's very easy to read a book a week. This habit contributed more to my knowledge base than my three university degrees. Over the following fifty-nine years, I've read about twenty-five hundred books, 80 per cent of which would be nonfiction.

My wealth-building corporate odyssey (see Appendix III for a summary) describes a journey in time and through places that were unique and will never occur again. The American West spanned a forty-year period from 1865 to 1905 and was a unique time of disease, loneliness, and nation building. It has been elevated to the status of a great, imagination-capturing myth. My equivalent period took place in Northern Nevada and Calgary and covered the thirty-year period from 1972 to 2002. The jet plane allowed me to inhabit the modern world of investment counselling and merchant banking while going on a magical ride four to five times a year, back to the Wild West of my youthful imagination. I liked to ski and play Texas hold 'em poker. I did this for twenty-four years in the Lake Tahoe Basin and Reno, Nevada, area and had many great adventures along with Nigel Martin, my late best friend. In 1982, a young financial analyst named Pierre Lassonde and I decided to create a business in the area where I had played. It changed our lives forever and created the fortune that led both of us to embark on the very ful-filling road of philanthropy.

This book is also aimed at the university students in the four Schulich Schools (Faculties) spread across Canada and at the Technion in Israel. A few of them might be curious about who their benefactor is and what lessons he might be able to convey to them as they go through the years of choosing a career path and a mate. In my experience, the years in age from twenty to thirty are, in many ways, the most difficult because of the search for direction in those two areas. After thirty, careers and the raising of families take over the attention of most young folks. The major objective of this book is to impart information I've acquired that might be relevant in the future, no matter what technological changes occur.

I have organized the chapters in an order such that material aimed at younger adults (or all readers in the case of "The Decision Maker") is presented in the early chapters. Toward the end, I get into material that's more suitable for the thirty-five- or forty-year-old reader who is already more established in business and in life. Younger readers may wish to skip the topics toward the end that are not relevant to their current lives or experience.

Many business or life lesson books leave you with two or three main ideas. My hope is that each reader who invests time and money in this book will leave with twenty to thirty ideas—and some that they can use to help transform or shape their lives.

I came across an inspirational message that sums up what my objective was in deciding to set up more than one thousand scholarships in six or seven institutions of higher learning, plus write a book to help young people deal with the major challenges of life's journey.

> A hundred years from now it will not matter what your bank account was, the sort of house you lived in, or the kind of car you drove...but the world may be different because you were important in the life of a young person.

My car is eleven years old, my marriage is thirty-eight years old, and my house is thirty years old. My current life objective is to be important and helpful in the lives of a lot of young people. This book is a part of the effort to achieve this major life goal.

May all the readers of this book be "forever young."

Seymour Schulich, C.M.

"Let's see ... one decision times 42 levels of management.
I should be able to get back to you in 18 months."

CHAPTER 1

THE DECISION-MAKER: A TOOL FOR A LIFETIME

If you learn nothing else from this book, the Decision-Maker will be worth the cover price a thousand times over. I learned this tool in a practical mathematics course more than fifty years ago and have used it for virtually every major decision of my adult life. It has never let me down and it will serve you well, too.

You've probably made a pro-and-con list for some big move in your life—which school to go to, whether or not to accept a job offer, and so on. The Decision-Maker adds a twist to this ancient concept. Here's how it works.

On one sheet of paper, list all the positive things you can about the issue in question, then give each one a score from zero to ten—the higher the score, the more important it is to you.

On another sheet, list the negative points, and score them from zero to ten—only this time, ten means it's a major drawback. Suppose you are thinking of buying a house, and you tour one that's in your price range, except the owners have painted every room to look like a giant banana. If you really hate yellow and can't stand the thought of lifting a paintbrush, you might give "ugly yellow house" a ten, and if it's not that big a deal, maybe a two or a three.

Then you add up the scores on each sheet. If the positive score is at least double the negative score, you should do it—whatever "it" is. But if the positives don't outweigh the negatives by that two-to-one ratio, don't do it, or at least think twice about it.

Yes, it is ridiculously easy. But one of the great fallacies of modern life is that decision-making has to be complicated to be effective. (It's a belief that's pervasive in the business world—many corporations are plagued by "analysis paralysis.") When I presented the Decision-Maker to an MBA class at the Schulich School of Business at York University, one student said it was far too simple to be taught by the quantitative professors who rule today's universities.

The Decision-Maker is designed not to allow one or two factors to sway a major life decision in a disproportionate way. It forces you strip away the emotion and really examine the relative importance of each point—which, of course, is why it works so well.

Let's illustrate the Decision-Maker with a relatively simple life choice—Should I go to an out-of-town university? When I was twenty-three years old, I was accepted at two excellent business schools—at University of Western Ontario's, in London, and McGill University's, which offered a new MBA program in my hometown of Montreal. Here's how I made the call:

EXAMPLE 1: SHOULD I GO TO WESTERN?

THE POSITIVES	POINTS
1. Having never studied or worked out of town, going to a new place would expand my life skills.	10
2. I was leaving no romantic attachments.	5
3. Western was the oldest established Canadian MBA school. It had a great reputation and a proven staff of professors.	8
Positive Score	**23 points**

THE NEGATIVES   POINTS

1. Money was a factor. Living at home meant   **8**
   not diluting the student experience by having
   to work.

2. McGill, while new and an unknown in faculty   **8**
   and reputation, was doing theory the first year
   and cases the second year. Western was all cases.
   I had a science degree and lacked the confidence
   to do all cases. I wanted the theory behind
   finance, accounting, statistics, and marketing.

3. McGill had few candidates with any business   **10**
   experience. Although I had a poor undergraduate
   grade record marred by an unsuccessful stint as
   an honours chemist, they were offering me a
   $1,600 scholarship against fees of $500.

4. McGill was drawing students from all over   **0**
   the world due to its international reputation.
   The networking possibilities should be as good
   as Western's.

Negative Score   **26 points**

As you can see, there were not enough positives to merit going to Western in London, Ontario, over staying put and being part of McGill's first MBA class.

It worked out beautifully. The professors at McGill, all six of them, had taken off a year and done nothing but prepare and incorporate the latest thinking into the McGill MBA curriculum. This program, under the leadership of dynamic new dean Don Armstrong, compressed eight years of experience into two years of study.

I turned the $1,600 scholarship into $5,000 with stock market investments in a junior oil company and a junior chemical company. I used my new wealth to tour Europe on $5 a day—which, based on the famous book of the day, was actually easy to do. I went for ninety days, covered ten countries, and spent $1,200, including all air and rail fares. For twenty-one days I stayed in Spain at a brand-new, four-star hotel in Majorca, with three excellent meals a day and a beautiful suite, for a total cost of $150. The place was so cheap, I thought about dropping out and living in Spain forever. To quote the great playwright Neil Simon: "I don't know whether those years were great or were great because we were young."

I grew on that trip and in the McGill MBA program, and it all started with the Decision-Maker. From that point on, for every key decision in my life, I used this tool to guide me—whether joining two budding financiers (Austin Beutel and Ned Goodman) to start an investment counselling business or leaving it twenty-two years later to run a junior mining company with Pierre Lassonde.

It can work for groups, too. When we were considering whether to sell our royalty company, Franco-Nevada, to Newmont Mining, Franco's executive team produced a collective Decision-Maker. We listed all the pros and cons, then the top four executives assigned their own point scores to each. We averaged them, the positives far outweighed the negatives, and we sold the company.

Does the Decision-Maker work? I have more than $1 billion in assets that says it sure does!

EXAMPLE 2: SHOULD I TAKE THAT JOB OFFER?

THE POSITIVES	POINTS
1. The salary is higher than my current job.	6
2. The company that's making the offer is a large, well-known firm where there is a lot of potential to advance and develop my career.	8

3. My future co-workers seem like a smart group, and my boss would be someone who is highly regarded in the field.   **8**

4. The job involves moving to a new city where we can be closer to family, and my spouse is very keen on the idea.   **10**

Positive Score   **32 points**

THE NEGATIVES   **POINTS**

1. I would be leaving behind colleagues I know and respect at a growing company where there's minimal bureaucracy and a bright future.   **8**

2. Real estate is more expensive and the cost of living is higher in the new city, offsetting some of the benefit of the better pay.   **5**

Negative Score   **13 points**

The proposition is more than 2:1 for the positives—therefore, take the job!

"I'm also very skilled at data storage."

CHAPTER 2

KNOW YOUR EDGE

I always ask aspiring businesspeople: How do you beat Bobby Fischer, the renowned chess champion of the 1970s?

The answer: Play him at anything but chess.

Always ask, where do I have the edge? History is replete with examples of big business mistakes that could have been avoided if only the people in charge had answered that simple question. It happens even at the biggest of companies. Coca-Cola veered into businesses like shrimp farming and plastics and even movies (in the early 1980s, Coke owned Columbia Pictures). Bell Canada diversified into financial services and real estate, among other things. Gillette began making digital watches and went exploring for oil. Mobil, the giant

American energy company that really *was* skilled at finding oil, branched out into furniture retailing.

All of these ventures went sour because the people running them had no advantage, no natural edge. It's extraordinarily difficult for most mortals to develop expertise in several very different areas. There are exceptions: Jack Welch, the iconic former CEO of General Electric, may be one example. But even Welch insisted that GE try to be first or second in any business in which it operated—large enough to give it an edge over the competition.

The know-your-edge principle also applies to the details of running a business. Take financing: When you go into a bank to borrow money, it's their lawyers who have drawn up the contract. It always has a clause that says, in essence: "No matter what you do, we can ask for our money back on any one of these (too numerous to count) pretexts in this completely incomprehensible document." When you borrow from a bank, they have the edge.

When you raise equity money from the public, you have the edge. The legal contract is between your group and a fee-hunting underwriter who, unless they are incompetent, ends up owning none of the shares. The public who buys the shares are never a part of the negotiations. They're not in the room when the terms are set.

In any deal, always try to have your lawyers write the contract. It's like having the serve in tennis. It's a big edge!

"This is just our way of saying thank you
to our most loyal customers."

CHAPTER 3

RECIPROCITY

When I entered McGill's MBA program in 1963, the professors gave everyone in the class three book-reading lists. Problem was, there were only two or three copies of each book and thirty-seven students who wanted them. As soon as the lists came out, a cavalry charge of nerds stampeded for the library.

The solution was to get the reading list ahead of time and reserve the books before everyone else, but how? I hatched a plan with my then classmate Lawrence Bloomberg, a serious, persistent fellow (who grew to become my best friend). We went to the Laura Secord store and bought the biggest box of fine chocolate we could find—$5 for five pounds (the same box would probably cost about $50 today). We gave it to Miss Sears, the intimidating, no-nonsense woman who ran the library.

Now, we didn't know what was going to be on the next MBA reading list, but Miss Sears sure did. So when the herd of nerds next appeared, they were told the books were reserved for Schulich and Bloomberg. Our classmates could never figure out how we always seemed to have our names at the top of the waiting list. (Bloomberg, by the way, went on to become one of Canada's most formidable investment bankers and ran First Marathon, which he sold to National Bank in 1999. He is now perhaps the best charity fundraiser and hospital chairman in Canada.)

This small anecdote illustrates one of the most important concepts for a young person to learn, in business and in life: reciprocity. In simple terms, reciprocity is the idea that people have a very hard time saying no to someone who has done something, even a small favour, for them.

That may seem obvious but it is a surprisingly powerful psychological tool. American psychologist Dr. Robert Cialdini, in his book *Influence: The Psychology of Persuasion*, tells of a university professor who, as an experiment, sent Christmas cards to a group of strangers. Although the professor expected some reaction, "the response he received was amazing—holiday cards addressed to him came pouring back from the people who had never met nor heard of him," Cialdini writes.

I first learned about Cialdini's book from Charlie Munger, the older partner of Warren Buffett and vice chairman of Berkshire Hathaway. *Influence* deals with the latest thinking on human psychology, with an emphasis on reciprocity, and it is a must-read book for young people, in my opinion. The entire business world, and much of family life, runs on relationships that are grounded in reciprocity. I've never met a successful person who didn't have a complete grasp of this.

Of course, sometimes reciprocity can go wrong, as my friend later learned. During an investor mining tour of Nevada, some of the players took a detour and dragged an unsuspecting Mr. Bloomberg along. While at the bar of Nevada's biggest brothel, The Mustang Ranch (where the customer always comes first), Bloomberg was approached by a beautiful buxom lady who said to him, "I'll do anything you want for $200." (This was many years ago.) Bloomberg looked up from his drink and said, "Good, come paint my house!"

"Good morning. To learn if your job still exists, press one."

CHAPTER 4

CAREER LINES—JOBS TO SEEK AND THOSE TO AVOID

When I was in my early twenties, I wanted to be an engineer. A year of study at McGill University's engineering school cured me of that desire. I switched into chemistry, but it didn't agree with me, or rather, I didn't agree with it: I flunked out. So I went to a career counselling service, took a test, and was told I ought to become a salesman. One of the first job offers I ever received, in fact, was to sell products for a Chicago-based company that made nuclear medical supplies. (My grades as a chemist, apparently, were not the handicap I thought they would be.)

I wasn't sold on that job or on the career advice. What I really wanted to do, deep down, was analyze investments. The only problem was the field hadn't been invented yet. Well, it had, but this was the 1960s, and security analysis was still not exactly a mainstream career. But I knew I could do it because I'd been dabbling in it since I was a teenager. I caught a break when a fellow (who today is a good friend) named Bob Stewart hired me to be an analyst at the firm of Eastern Securities. I was twenty-five and intimidated, but I made it work and soon became a partner.

Why recount this ancient history? Because young people today often feel pressure to begin laying out their career paths as soon as they've got their first case of acne. In high school, they're told to take the right courses to get into the right university programs for the right jobs when they graduate.

In your teens and early twenties, you *should* be thinking about what you're going to do with your life. But you *shouldn't* freak out if the first couple of things you try don't work. That's natural. For every success story like Michael Dell, the entrepreneur who began building computers out of his college dormitory room, there are many more like Jeffrey Bezos, who worked at obscure financial jobs before starting Amazon.com at the age of thirty, or Ray Kroc, who was a travelling salesman of milkshake mixers when he stumbled across the idea that would make him famous— McDonald's.

Your twenties are a time for gaining the experience on which you will build the rest of your life. It doesn't matter all that much what you do, as long as it's legal. By thirty, though, you should have a clear direction. Only you can know where you'll find your niche; no career counselling service can tell you. In my opinion, a key is to find work in a business with high profit margins. These jobs usually pay more, have fewer layoffs and bankruptcies, plus are much less stressful.

Today's high-margin business is not always tomorrow's. The industrial development of China and India has created a boom in base metals and coal, industries that had lagged for twenty years. Conversely, pharmaceuticals, which used to be the best of high-margin businesses, are being squeezed by generic drug firms.

In general, I would avoid:

- airlines
- auto parts
- retailing
- biotechnology
- grocery stores
- chemicals
- wholesaling
- machinery manufacturing
- paper and forest products

- auto manufacturing
- restaurants
- appliance manufacturing
- trucking
- any manufacturing competing with China
- telecom services

Don't misunderstand: You may be able to find fulfillment and a rewarding career in any of the above. But you're more likely to find satisfaction and superior financial rewards in industries with superior economics.

Doctors and lawyers get paid by the visit or hour. Therefore, their pay is limited to the number of hours in a day. You can make a very good living at these professions. However, you will never get truly rich being paid by the hour with a 50 per cent marginal tax rate.

"What's this part where the money grows wings and flies away?"

CHAPTER 5

MONEY'S VALUE FALLS 90 PER CENT EVERY THIRTY YEARS

The Roman leaders of two thousand years ago learned that the key to popularity was free bread and circuses. Not much has changed. They don't build statues to honour cost-cutters, and as long as that's the case, politicians will print money to help pay for their promises, bringing inflation and debasing the value of a dollar. The older you get, the clearer this pattern becomes.

At the risk of reaping the ridicule that is heaped on rich folks who, while proficient at making money, have never learned how to spend it, here's a real-life illustration of inflation's effect. Not long ago, I decided to replace two old reliable possessions. The first was a wonderful pair of fur-lined leather boots that I had purchased in 1974 for $35. They had been resoled three times and finally wore out beyond repair. The second item was a reclining armchair I bought in 1972 for $200, so comfortable that I'd once rescued it from the garbage and had it reupholstered.

So I set out on a cold January day to find replacements for these old friends that had served me so well for more than thirty years. The new boots cost me $350, while my new buckskin leather armchair cost $2,000. In each case, the price was exactly ten times what it was three decades earlier, excluding all taxes. That's a 90 per cent change in the value of a dollar!

The emergence of China as a low-cost manufacturing power has slowed the devaluation of paper currencies, not stopped it. Even modest inflation quickly adds up to a big loss of purchasing power. Suppose you bought a car for $25,000 and drove it for a dozen years, during which there was inflation of 4 per cent annually. By the time you went shopping for a new one, the same model would cost $40,000.

Being aware of this fact will make you think about money differently. My advice:

1. *Keep a sizable proportion of your wealth in inflation-sensitive assets, like real estate, commodities, and precious metals.* They will hold their value against

the ravages of inflation far better than cash, bonds, GICs, or other long-term paper savings (see chapter 41).

2. *If you get the chance to lock in your debts for years at low rates of interest, do it.* Inflation is the saver's enemy but the debtor's friend. It cuts the burden of repaying borrowed money. Today, bankers and real estate brokers often advise young people to take short-term or floating mortgages that fluctuate with interest rates. Financing your home is cheaper this way, they'll tell you. But this piece of conventional "wisdom" has been formed in an era of falling inflation and interest rates—an era that won't last forever and is probably already over. Ask anyone who had to renew his or her mortgage in the early 1980s, at rates of fifteen to 20 per cent, how it feels to have short-term debt when interest costs are high and going higher.

3. *Be skeptical of life insurance.* Many insurance policies are simply overpriced savings plans in an insurance package. Inflation will destroy their value. If you're going to buy life insurance, buy term insurance, and get only as much as you need to protect your family in case something happens to you.

PRICE MILESTONES & EXPECTATIONS:
Comparison Of Prices: My Experiences as a Boy up to Today

Item	Price Then	Years Past	Price Today	Expected Price 2040
Stamp for a first-class letter	2¢	60	51¢	$5
Chocolate Bar	5¢	60	$1.25	$10
Ice Cream Cone	5¢	60	$2.00	$20
Bread (Loaf)	15¢	60	$3.00	$30
Gasoline (Gallon)	25¢	60	$3.00	$30+
First Car— New Price (1957 Ford Fairlane)	$1,700	50	$25,000	$200,000
Wife's Parents' House— Halifax, 1946	$4,500	60	$500,000	$2,500,000
Our House in Toronto, Built in 1973, Bought in 1977	$280,000	30	$1,200,000	$10,000,000

"I don't know why. I just felt like standing up
and shouting 'I've got great news!'"

CHAPTER 6

BE A POSITIVE PERSON

When I was eighteen years old, I took a summer job at a drug company. As student jobs went, this was a good one. The pay was decent, and work wasn't back-breaking: I stood in an office all day and wrapped packages for shipping.

About the fourth day on the job, while some of my colleagues were out on a lunch break, I decided to give my aching legs a rest and put my feet up on a desk for a few minutes. My boss wandered by, looked through the window, believed I was loafing, and fired me.

It's easy to laugh about it now, but at the time I felt humiliated. I was in university, I needed money, and I had just lost a plum gig. My father encouraged me to keep my chin up and to not delay looking for a new job—the sooner I began the search, the better. He was right, and even though the new job was a more difficult one (working in a glass factory), the sting of getting fired soon faded. I'd learned something about staying positive.

Losing that job, in the grand scheme of things, was a minor deal. Others have proved the power of a positive attitude in the face of far more devastating news. Katharine Graham, the woman who ran the *Washington Post* during the Watergate era, was a forty-six-year-old housewife when her husband, Phil, committed suicide in 1963. Even as she felt overwhelmed with grief, she was forced to take over the family company at a time when there were few women in senior positions anywhere in the corporate world. She was, in a word, terrified.

But Graham went on to lead a remarkable, fascinating life—in her new role, she came to know every president from Kennedy to Clinton. And though she was a novice in business, on her watch the Washington Post Co. became one of the most successful media groups in the United States, propelled by the reputation it acquired when it exposed Richard Nixon's role in the Watergate affair. How did she manage it, in a job she had never wanted and inherited only through personal tragedy? She gave credit to skilled managers, perseverance, and a positive attitude. "What I essentially did was to put one foot in front of the other, shut my eyes, and step off the edge," she later recalled.

Sometimes it takes only a small change in perspective to alter your attitude. For years I suffered through Canada's cloudy winter days. I had SAD (Seasonal Affective Disorder). Then one day I read *The Shadow of the Sun*, a book by Polish journalist Ryszard Kapuscinski, who spent many years in equatorial Africa. He wrote of dreadful heat, the sun erupting out of the ground each morning, half the people suffering malaria, and no shade anywhere as the few trees had been felled for fuel long ago. Then a thought struck him: "Do the inhabitants of the North appreciate what a treasure they possess in that grey, drab, perpetually cloudy sky, with its one great, miraculous advantage—that there is no sun in it?"

This was an epiphany. This Polish writer changed my entire view of our sunless northern winters. I had a complete attitude adjustment. Cloudy days no longer made me depressed. I just thought of those poor souls who live in equatorial Africa.

Virtually all the accomplished people I've known in my life had positive outlooks most of the time. Behind every success story is usually someone who beat the obstacles because he or she refused to accept the pessimist's view.

Accountants and lawyers are the major exceptions to this rule. There's something inherent in these professions that leads to dour, worst-case-scenario outlooks. I once asked Ron Binns, an accountant who has been an outstanding chief financial officer and a close associate for more than sixteen years, why that was so. His answer was thought-provoking and profound: "I became a pessimist by financing optimists."

Maybe every company needs a few people like Binns. But positive people form the vast majority of life's winners.

My parents told me, "Laugh and the world will laugh with you, cry and you cry alone."

Two men looked through prison bars,
One saw mud, one saw stars.

—*Oscar Wilde*

"My secret of success is redefining success."

CHAPTER 7

THERE'S NO SUCH THING AS AN OVERNIGHT SUCCESS

Howard Schultz thought he had a great business idea, but everywhere he went, he was running into walls. In need of more than a million dollars to get it off the ground, he approached two hundred forty-two people for money. Two hundred and seventeen turned him down. Some told him he was crazy, that it would never work, that he should quit wasting his time and "just go get a job."*

The year was 1986. His idea? A chain of upscale coffee bars—better known today as Starbucks.

Schultz's pipe dream now has more than ten thousand outlets in thirty-seven countries. It has one in

* Schultz himself related this story in his autobiography, *Pour Your Heart Into It*.

the Forbidden City in China. Soon it will have them in Russia, India, and Brazil, three of the world's most promising emerging markets. Starbucks is one of the five most admired companies in America, according to a *Fortune* magazine survey, and Schultz made multi-millionaires out of the people who had faith in his early vision. But it took time. Starbucks *seems* like a rapid success to those who've casually watched it open new stores all around us. In reality, Schultz began working on the concept in 1982 and sweated over it for a decade before it went public and became an international success.

That's typical: It usually takes five to ten years to build a successful business, even in industries like oil or mining, where quick strikes can happen. Franco-Nevada existed for four years and participated in forty-three different exploration plays, most of them unsuccessful, before it bought the royalties on the Nevada property that would lead to its first windfall. Franco lasted for twenty years; that's also a typical lifespan for a corporation. In his book, *The Living Company*, former Shell executive Arie de Geus said that one-third of the companies on the 1970 Fortune 500 list had disappeared thirteen years later. The average life expectancy of a multinational company was forty to fifty years.

Nothing lasts forever, and great businesses aren't created in a few weeks or months. An Italian proverb says, "He that has no patience has nothing at all." Wise words for aspiring entrepreneurs.

CHAPTER 8

RULES FOR AGING (OR LIVING)

Most of the lessons you'll see in these pages are things I learned from direct experience. But anyone, of any age, can also learn from listening to the wisdom of others. In the introduction I told you that I've read about twenty-five hundred books in my lifetime; one of the most important is a wonderful little paperback called *Rules for Aging* by Roger Rosenblatt.

This philosophical gem is aimed at people more than sixty years of age, and in my opinion it's a bit too cynical for young folks. But many of Rosenblatt's rules are extremely useful, no matter what your age, because they deal with something that never changes—human nature. Here are a few examples:

1. *Nobody is thinking about you.* So much energy is wasted on worrying that your professor hates you, or your boss is out to get you, or your roommate/boyfriend thinks you're getting soft around the middle (and doing a few situps every now and again wouldn't kill you, now, would it?). Liberate yourself. Banish paranoid thoughts from your mind. Rosenblatt says: "I promise you: Nobody is thinking about you. They are thinking about themselves—just like you." (And in the unlikely event that your boss really is out to get you—well, spending your nights fretting about it isn't going to help very much, is it?)

2. *Avoid swine* (people who act in a swine-like fashion). It's worth buying this fine book just to understand this rule for a less stressful life. "A swine is a swine is a swine," says Rosenblatt—and a swine will always be a swine, even if, for the moment, he is acting in an unswine-like fashion. You cannot reform swine. It's better just to stay away from them.

3. *Appearance is frequently reality.* No matter what they told you in university.

4. *Envy no one—ever* (see Chapter 15).

5. *After the age of thirty, it is unseemly to blame one's parents for one's life.* This rule is self-explanatory, but easily violated.

6 *Never bring news of slander to a friend.* This goes against conventional wisdom, which says a true friend is one with the guts to break bad news to a pal. In this case, conventional wisdom is wrong. When a friend hears a slander from an enemy, he or she automatically discounts it as meaningless; but when it comes from a friend, says Rosenblatt, "his guard is down, and he is vulnerable." Hey, there's a reason that in ancient times messengers were often beheaded.

7. *Never expect gratitude.* This may seem overly negative, but it's actually quite practical. This rule is really an extension of the nobody's-thinking-about-you dictum. If you spend your life expecting glory and praise for the good things you do, you are going to burn a lot of energy and time fuming when gratitude doesn't come your way. So don't expect it, and you'll feel pleasantly surprised when someone does express thanks.

SELF-PRAISE IS NO HONOUR

Perhaps the most valuable rule for aging and life stemmed from my wife, Tanna, whom I've known for forty years. "Self-praise is no honour." Besides acquainting me with this great truth (many, many times), she has practiced it religiously.

Think about this rule! If you say you're great, you're a braggart, a bore, or someone people will flee from at any party or gathering. However, if another person says you're great, people pay attention and are at least intrigued by the possibility.

One of my favourite definitions is that of an all-American football player: "He is a fellow with two good blockers and a poet in the press box." The poet in the press box has created many legends—from Jesse James and the outlaws of the Wild West to the fields of athletics and business. A key to success is to have friends and colleagues who will remind the world of your achievements. Never, ever do it yourself.

"That was the cigarette-smoke detector."

CHAPTER 9

LONGEVITY AND HEALTH

With aging comes a changing goal,
and one that's most bemusing,
no longer is it how to win,
but how to keep from losing.

As we age, various health problems assail us, our friends, and family. I have read well over a hundred books on various specialized health topics. I have endowed a Heart Center and a Medical School, which have brought me into contact with numerous skilled medical practitioners. I've also mentored a young genius on his entire path through medical school and into practice.

I've come through surgery that dealt with potential issues of both mortality and severe impairment to some of life's critical functions.

A family member underwent a sixteen-hour siege in an emergency room, during which one of my most revered medical friends disclosed the following items:

(A) In 50 per cent of the cases entering emergency rooms, no conclusion is reached as to the cause of the problem.

(B) Only 10 per cent of doctors are truly competent. (This should not have come as a big surprise to me as only 10 per cent of security analysts, money managers, geologists, and other professionals we are familiar with could be classified as world beaters.)

So what are the main conclusions about longevity and health that I wish to pass on to the twenty- to forty-year-old target group?

1. Studious folks (nerds of which the author is certainly one) suffer much less wear and tear than the athletic jocks of our high school and college years.

2. A good measure of how long you're going to live is the ages your parents attained.

3. Health and longevity can be enhanced by doing two things:

   (A) Exercise: Aerobically, three times a week. Strength training, twice a week.

   (B) Don't smoke.
   If you want to die ten to twenty years before your time, smoking is the way to do it.

4. A risk in young folks (especially women) is an obsession with mythical diseases they may be carrying or risk contracting. My advice is do not study diseases unless you're going to be a doctor. There's a great expression I picked up from a young person: "That's more information than I need to know or want to know." There are a lot of diseases and health demons out there that you do not want to know or obsess about. Deal only with the issues directly affecting you and your family. You will have a better life if you avoid life's health issues until you have to confront them. The Internet provides an infinite amount of information when you are required to cope with a specific health issue.

5. Keeping yourself mentally stimulated is very important—maybe even critical—to a long life.

That's usually not a problem for most young people, but it can become a trap for anyone who achieves early success and wealth and is tempted to give it up for life on the golf course. (One of the greatest mining executives I ever knew did this and died within two years—of boredom.) "Retirement at sixty-five is ridiculous," comedian George Burns once said. "When I was sixty-five I still had pimples." May you be so blessed.

6. Handling bereavement or the loss of people close to you is a must for people who reach extreme age. Personally, I fear this life test the most.

On nutrition: I had two parents who contracted colon cancer. If you survived the Depression, eating red meat three to four times a week was a mark of success. In my opinion, it's the primary cause of colon cancer.

CHAPTER 10

PATIENCE: A KEY TO SUCCESS IN BUSINESS AND LIFE

I played Texas hold 'em poker in Nevada for twenty-five years before the game became the Internet and television phenomenon of this generation. It was fun and taught me to be patient. Top players usually play only 5 to 10 per cent of the hands they're dealt. Without patience, you can't win at either poker or business.

People who win at business bet seldom and only when the odds are in their favour. Winners put themselves in a position of seeing a very large range of potential investments. Then they buy into or invest in perhaps one out of a hundred opportunities. The career lines that provide this much exposure are venture capital or merchant banking. Warren Buffett states you need a maximum of twenty great insights in a lifetime to become very wealthy and successful.

Buffett has a great analogy to encourage patience in business and investing: it's like a baseball game in which there are no called strikes. You can stand at the plate and watch pitch after pitch go by, and swing at only the ones you think you can knock out of the park. One other very important aspect of patience in business is maintaining a cash reserve, so you have the money on hand to exploit those opportunities when they occur.

Academics are beginning to examine what Buffett knows intuitively to be true. One such study took one hundred adults from a remote tribe of Amerindians in Bolivia. Each was asked to choose from three options: get a small amount of food or money now, get a larger amount in a week, or wait several months for an even larger reward. Five years later, the academics returned; they found that the volunteers who were the most patient in the original experiment had enjoyed the fastest growth in their incomes.

Despite the evidence that patience really is a virtue, over and over again I see people rush into business mistakes, not only in big corporations but in the smallest ones. A lot of people view running their own business as the key to economic freedom. They'll save for many years then plunge into a local restaurant, store, or motel. These are low-margin, immobile businesses that have long working hours and high failure rates. These folks are not exposed to enough investment opportunities and usually fail to take the time to do enough market research on the propositions they place their bets on. They often spend most of their lives paying off the debts their entrepreneurial zeal racked up.

The investment industry is also rife with impatience. If one strategy isn't doing well at the moment, mutual fund sellers will quickly invent new products to take advantage of what is. (This is how billions of dollars in investors' capital were sucked into overvalued technology stocks at the end of the 1990s.) Buffett's eighty-three-year-old partner, a wise man named Charlie Munger, has a very instructive anecdote that he shared with students at the University of Southern California in a 1994 speech, and which was published in the book *Poor Charlie's Almanack*:

> To me, it's obvious that the winner has to bet very selectively. It's been obvious to me since very early in life. I don't know why it's not obvious to very many other people.
>
> I think the reason why we got into such idiocy in investment management is best illustrated by a story that I tell about the guy who sold fishing

tackle. I asked him, "My God, they're purple and green. Do fish really take these lures?" And he said, "Mister, I don't sell to fish."

Investment managers are in the position of that fishing tackle salesman. They're like the guy who was selling salt to the guy who already had too much salt. And as long as the guy will buy salt, why they'll sell salt. But that isn't what ordinarily works for the buyer of investment advice.

CHAPTER 11

SUCCESS CORRELATES TO EXPOSURE

The old saying is true: fortune really does favour the bold.
But it also favours the person who participates in
many endeavours. A lot of the great things that happened to me did so because I kept my hand in a lot of
different ventures. I've invested in more than fifteen
small oil companies over the years, in each case as
either a key shareholder or director. We were
involved in nearly four dozen exploration plays at
Franco-Nevada before we hit on the formula that created one of the great Canadian resource investment
stories, turning a $1,000 investment into $1.25 million over nineteen years. We tried and tried, and
failed and failed, then found success beyond our
wildest imagination.

This doesn't mean you should ignore my earlier advice to play where you think you have an edge (see Chapter 2) and be patient (see Chapter 10). Through most of my career I focused on investing in companies in oil, natural gas, and mining. That was a strong suit I developed over time, and as I became more comfortable in it, I tried to gain a wide exposure to different business opportunities within that group. (When I moved out of this realm—by investing in start-up biotechnology companies, for instance—the results were often poor.)

Many successful people arrived at their niche in life through exposure and experimentation in areas that interested them. Charles Schwab had an interest in the stock market and ran an investment newsletter for a while. That venture did not give him the success he was after, but it undoubtedly helped him formulate an idea that would help popularize stock investing among the masses. Charles Schwab Corp. is today the biggest discount brokerage firm in the world.

Steve Case worked for Procter & Gamble and Pizza Hut; selling shampoo and pepperoni pies didn't excite him, but the experience he gained developing products and marketing them to the masses proved valuable when he was building America Online in the early days of the Internet.

Ted Turner spent his teenage years working at his father's billboard company. He came to know every part of the business—sales, leases, construction, even painting billboards. His exposure to the advertising business taught him it had terrific potential beyond billboards; he created CNN and a broadcasting empire.

Fred Smith started a small music company, flew airplanes for a charter service, and served in the Marine Corps in Vietnam. His exposure to the air transport business and to the military, with its emphasis on structure and chain of command, gave him what he needed to start a shipping company built on the principle of ruthless efficiency—Federal Express. I like Smith's story because, like mine, it has a Nevada connection: in the early 1970s, when his new enterprise was struggling financially, he flew to Las Vegas on a lark and won $27,000 at the blackjack table. The money helped FedEx get through a temporary cash crunch, and Smith took it as an omen to persevere.

Some call him lucky. I say he showed the qualities—guts, moxie, patience, persistence, self-confidence—that entrepreneurs are made of. And I'd guess that he had some of those things in part because of the wide variety of experience he gathered up as a young man. It helped him figure out his edge.

"This thing? It's been running in the basement forever. Why do you ask?"

CHAPTER 12

HANDLING ADVERSITY: LIFE LESSON

It's easy enough to be cheerful when life flows
　　along like a song
but the person who is worthwhile is the person
　　with a smile
when everything goes dead wrong.

—Ella Wheeler Wilcox

That poem was handed down, along with a plethora of street smarts and wisdom, by my beloved father, Julius. Many a time I would recite it when adversity beset me. It was a mental lifesaver. Its origin was unknown to him and the saying was acquired during his early years of a life that went from 1898 to 1985.

He was married to my mother, Bessie, for sixty years. Born in New York, he came up to Canada in 1914, joined the Royal Canadian Field Artillery, and fought four years in Europe in World War I.

After their marriage at age twenty-six, my parents moved to New York.

In 1932, my father lost his job in the Depression. My parents had a three-year-old daughter and were living off the wages of my mother, who was an executive secretary. Adversity struck: their life savings of $3,000 (about $300,000 in today's dollars) were lost when the Bank of the United States closed down because its mortgage portfolio was beset with defaults spawned by the Depression (24 per cent unemployment).

That one event created financial insecurity that scarred their lives forever. Imagine all your savings, credit cards, cash cards, and access to any cash just disappear. It's back to living paycheque to paycheque, except your jobs just disappeared too. That was the recurring scenario for the generation who lived through the Depression of 1929 to 1939. There was no welfare system or unemployment insurance at the time.

NINETY PER CENT OF WHAT YOU WORRY ABOUT NEVER HAPPENS

Usually the negative things in life that befall you are things you have never thought about at all. The 10 per cent of the worries that materialize are rarely as bad as your anxious mind envisioned.

My father dealt me this great piece of wisdom.

ANOTHER LESSON ON ADVERSITY

While on a cruise, my wife, Tanna, and I landed for a tour of a small trading post island called Samandor off Papua New Guinea. The whole island covered about a thousand acres. We, as was our custom, split off from the group and proceeded to hike around and into the centre of this mini heart of darkness.

In the middle of the island, we came across an eighteen-foot-high black granite obelisk with the following inscription:

Life is mostly froth and bubbles,
but two things stand like stone,
aid to a friend in trouble and courage in your
own.

This was the dedication to a thirty-one-year-old British missionary who was killed by the natives in 1905. (It was written by Adam Lindsay Gordon, Australian author, 1833–1870.) It seems the missionary was invited to dinner by the local folks without perusing the menu, which would have disclosed that he was the dinner. What a wonderful epitaph to help people cope with the adversity of ill health in their friends, relatives, and themselves.

You must always have more dreams than
memories!

—Thomas L. Friedman, *The World Is Flat*

"And the award for the most presumptuous
egoist in the world goes to . . ."

CHAPTER 13

SEX AND LOVE

Sex was put on this earth to make fools of people, and it does all the time.

Not all great brains have a penis attached.

Businesspeople have four enemies. Every fall from grace, every personal crack-up or failure invariably can be traced back to one or more of the following four causes:

1. *Ego:* This one destroys more people than any other single thing.

2. *Greed:* In an Aesop fable, a dog with a lamb chop crosses a stream and sees his reflection. Thinking it's a chance to grab a second chop, the dog opens

his mouth and lunges at the reflected lamb chop. In the process, he drops the one he has, and the current sweeps it away. His greed leaves him with nothing!

3. *Alcohol and drugs:* These two weaknesses or diseases destroy many an executive career.

4. *Assistants with big breasts:* They can destroy many careers, fortunes, families, and marriages. The late, great Jimmy Goldsmith (European financier) once said, "If you want to create a new job, marry your mistress." He should have known—he did this several times.

A golden rule learned during fifty years of observation: Don't take spouses or "significant others" to business meetings out of town or on tours. They're not interested. They tend to be a giant distraction. They can create havoc through poor interaction with other executives.

Women are wired differently and, in many ways, have an edge on males in both priorities and leadership abilities.

In their priorities as mothers and grandmothers, women nurture the next generation in a dedicated manner superior to the male warriors who are out hunting, gathering, and building estates and businesses.

Males grow up in a world where having a chip on their shoulder is a bit of a positive. In a hockey game, if they get slashed, they wait and retaliate in the corners with a butt-end to an opponent's head or, if the opponent is a blockhead, other tender parts of his body. Women don't have this chippy, macho edge. The women university presidents I've had the privilege to know and work with, Dr. Lorna Marsden and Dr. Heather Munroe-Blum, are outstanding leaders and human beings who brought out the really important values in human relations: abundant respect and loyalty!

This leads us to love.

LOVE

Love is a hormonal imbalance that usually occurs in our twenties. If we are lucky, we outgrow it. It should evolve into respect and loyalty, which are the real foundations for a long-term relationship.

MARRIAGE—TWO RULES FOR A HAPPY UNION

1. Live and let live, or, never try to change the other person.

2. Never argue in front of other people (including children).

Dr. Dan Baker,* the resident psychologist at the Canyon Ranch in Tucson, whom I've known for seventeen years, taught me one of life's great truths and lessons: "The only thing you can really control is your own behaviour!" Stop trying to control your relatives, friends, partners, employees, and so on—it will just make you unhappy.

AN IMPORTANT POEM ABOUT RELATIONSHIPS

You are you
And I am I,
If by chance we find each other—it's beautiful
If not—it can't be helped.
I do my thing,
You do your thing.

*Author of *What Happy People Know*.

I am not in this world to live
up to your expectations
And you are not in this world to
live up to mine.

—Fritz Perls

P.S. This chapter contains the views of an old (very rich) dinosaur. It is for better or worse what he's observed over a lifetime. It could well be the world has changed. It could be as time passes some of these observations may tally with your own life experience. It may be that your experiences never validate my observations.

For better or worse it's what *this* one old man observed. His motto is: "Often wrong, but never in doubt."

"Ms. Donovan, hire me two friends."

CHAPTER 14

FRIENDS

Real relationships are built up over twenty-, thirty-, and forty-year time periods. My wise, street-smart father told me I would be very lucky to have two close friends in my lifetime outside my family. His rule for defining a friend is someone who would loan you $10,000 (that's about $100,000 in today's dollars). From the perspective of age sixty-six, I realize Dad was right. At this stage, I don't have the years left to form really close friendships.

Partners share a common interest when they're building something together. They always command a very special place in one's heart and thoughts. Ex-partners often move on to new ventures with their families, especially if sons are involved.

Usually, mavens (see *The Tipping Point* by Malcolm Gladwell) make close friends with connectors or salesmen. That has been the case in my life.

One friendship that lasted forty years featured a man who had very unique attributes worth examining. Let's keep his anonymity by calling him Harry. Now, Harry came up through the military, retired at forty-two years old after attaining a high rank and serving several years in Canadian Intelligence in Washington. Everybody, male and female, liked this man. Why?

Harry made a lot of his contacts by inviting people to fishing camps in Newfoundland and Labrador. He and a rather colourful Newfoundland best friend entertained countless businessmen, premiers, prime ministers, and US presidents at these camps. There's no better way to learn about people than spending three days trapped in a fishing camp with them. This setting sifts out the alcoholics, the frivolous, the smart, the dumb, and generally exposes most personality flaws and attributes.

Harry showed all his guests great respect. Each one was made to feel he or she was important. When Harry spoke to a person, his eyes didn't dart around the room seeking more important folks to buttonhole. The person he was talking to was the centre of his world (at that moment). He never talked about himself or his family. He always talked about the other person, his or her interests, views, business, and what investments he or she thought might possess some merit.

Although a very successful businessman, he lived fairly simply. (His only toys were a thirteen-year-old Ferrari and a maroon fedora.) At his fishing camps, he was the leader and puppet master. He manoeuvred people around without their being aware of it. He never bragged, was an excellent host, and engendered great respect from virtually all the staff and employees.

We often went on cruise ships together. He and his wife used tea time to get to know a lot of fellow travellers. I considered that to be a waste of time. Not deterred, every day, he trolled the tea lounge and invariably knew all the key players on board.

The fascinating thing about Harry was how he could bond with people in a short period of time. He probably never read Dale Carnegie, yet used all the techniques in the book *How to Win Friends and Influence People*. I've never met a man respected and beloved by more people. I'm still trying to analyze how he does it.

CHAPTER 15

NEVER ENVY THE RICH MAN OR ANY PERSON

My father often said he'd give me all his money to be my age.
When I was young, it was hard to comprehend this
desire. Today, at sixty-seven, it's crystal clear. In my
case, aging has meant gaining more wealth but being
able to do less. First went tennis (tennis elbow), then
skiing (tendonitis and a desire to save legs for hiking). Finally, my beloved hiking ability has fallen
from Level 4 to Level 2 at the Canyon Ranch in
Tucson where my wife and I have visited annually
for twenty-five years.

If you're twenty to thirty years old, you have
energy, a keen, young, inquiring mind, and the bulk of
your life's journey ahead of you. You are blessed to be
living in a time of the Internet and the communication

it creates. Human lifespans are increasing. Health care has never been better. Transportation to anywhere on the planet is relatively cheap and easily available.

Use these advantages. Don't waste time on what you don't have. Never envy the old rich man and never envy your peers. Besides, the people you are jealous of might not be as they appear. When I was in university, the president of the student society was a popular fellow in law school. He came from a wealthy family, had the prettiest girls, and was the envy of every introverted, studious nerd on campus (myself included). One year after graduating magna cum laude, he committed suicide.

Five years later, this great lesson was reinforced by a folk song on the hit album *Sounds of Silence* by Simon and Garfunkel. The song was called "Richard Cory" and was written by Paul Simon, who derived it from a poem written by Edwin A. Robinson.

RICHARD CORY

They say that Richard Cory owns one half of this
   whole town
With political connections to spread his wealth
   around.
Born into society, a banker's only child,

He had everything a man could want: power,
  grace, and style.

But I work in his factory
And I curse the life I'm living
And I curse my poverty
And I wish that I could be,
Oh, I wish that I could be,
Oh, I wish that I could be
Richard Cory.

The papers print his picture almost everywhere he
  goes:
Richard Cory at the opera, Richard Cory at a
  show.
And the rumor of his parties and the orgies on his
  yacht!
Oh, he surely must be happy with everything he's
  got.

But I work in his factory
And I curse the life I'm living
And I curse my poverty
And I wish that I could be,
Oh, I wish that I could be,
Oh, I wish that I could be
Richard Cory.

He freely gave to charity, he had the common
touch,
And they were grateful for his patronage and
thanked him very much,
So my mind was filled with wonder when the
evening headlines read:
"Richard Cory went home last night and put a
bullet through his head."

"You look like the smart and handsome kind of person who will
sign a contract without even looking at it. Am I right?"

CHAPTER 16

BE THE PROMOTER, NOT THE PROMOTEE (OR PATSY)

They say in a poker game if you can't figure out who the weak players (patsies) are at the table within thirty minutes then you're the patsy.

I made T-shirts that stated, "I was not put on this earth to be promoted by other people." Many hustlers will start companies and buy founder's stock at ten cents a share then peddle stock to you at $1 to $2 a share. Who's going to get rich? The guy who buys the ten-cent stock or you?

One of the worst forms of promotion foisted on consumers in our society is the credit card. The banks charge eighteen to 22 per cent interest on unpaid balances, plus far above market rates of currency conversion on purchases made in foreign countries.

Merchants are charged 3 to 5 per cent when buyers use credit cards. If you use these cards, pay them promptly or keep credit balances in these accounts to avoid this modern form of usury or loan sharking.

Franchising has made a lot of people rich (namely, the folks who sell the franchises). It's also made a lot of people either poor or the equivalent of slaves (often the buyers of franchises, who are the promotees). In this game, the seller's lawyer draws up all the rules to protect the seller (promoter). The buyer (promotee) often uses no counsel. Whose rights are protected?

If you buy a franchise, talk to at least five people who have dealt with the franchisor and presumably had a happy experience. Learn what pitfalls they encountered and if they would do it again.

One way to succeed in life is to copy successful ideas that other promoters exploit. There are no patents on good business ideas. The only advantage they confer on the originators is a longer lead time than is available to the imitators.

Every profession is a conspiracy against lay people. If you hire management consultants, make them explain why they're right. My advice is, don't hire management consultants—you're the promotee!

Auctions manipulate people into completely irrational and ego-driven behaviour. The definition of the term "winner's curse" is to be the high bidder in an auction. Avoid them! You're the promotee!

All promoters follow a few golden rules:

(A) They never let the facts get in the way of a really good story.

(B) The one-eyed man (the promoter) is king in the land of the blind (among lay people).

(C) Even a blind squirrel finds an acorn now and then.

In the old days in Nevada, the ladies at the Mustang Ranch, who were promoters of lust, used to say to departing customers, "It's a business doing pleasure with you."

"Please hold for ten minutes while I transfer you to the Lost Sale Department."

CHAPTER 17

SELLING

Sooner or later everybody has to sell something. You could be selling yourself, a product, a project, a charity, or an institution or company with which you're associated. I was never a professional salesman, but over the years I picked up a few tools that helped me enormously in this area.

(A) *Once you have made a sale, stop selling*

I learned this lesson from an old, successful, and delightful stockbroker named Nat Sandler. Too often an entrepreneur/salesperson will have the sale made and then proceed to undo it by talking too much.

(B) *Never bring bad news to clients*

I knew a security salesman who knew the holdings of clients. When a positive event occurred, such as increased earnings or dividends, he called. Conversely, he never called to convey any bad developments. The result was the customers grew to welcome his calls, whereas other salesmen never got their foot in the door.

(C) *Don't point out hypocrisy*

My senior partner, the very wise Austin Beutel, once told me that people generally don't appreciate having their hypocrisy dramatically pointed out. This is especially true of the establishment or rich folks. This lesson was administered to me after I had bent Austin's ear for about fifteen minutes concerning some blatant hypocrites in our community.

(D) *It's a fine line between being persistent and being a pest*

Try to know when to back off.

"My wish, not yours."

CHAPTER 18

NEVER GIVE OUT FREE OPTIONS

Not long ago, I was involved with the board of a junior oil producer. For years, this company had held a large, uneconomic heavy-oil deposit. (Heavy oil, as the name suggests, is a form of crude oil that does not flow as freely as light crude, and therefore costs more to pump and refine.) They had put in a pilot production system but, because oil prices were low, they were losing small amounts of money running it.

One of the directors approached the company and negotiated a free three-month option to buy this asset for $35 million, if he could raise the money. I objected. If oil prices rose during the three-month window and the project turned profitable, he'd raise the money and take it from us for $35 million. And if that didn't happen, well, there was no risk to him: he didn't have the obligation to buy anything. This arrangement was clearly worth something. Why should the company give it to him for nothing?

This is what I mean in this chapter by an "option": it's the right to buy something (usually an asset) at a specific price at some point in the future. Options aren't evil; they're an integral part of modern capitalism. A developer might buy an option on a vacant parcel of land, believing that he could put an apartment building there eventually. A private company might give a new partner an option to own a piece of the business later on. In the case of the oil company, the error wasn't in granting my fellow director the option on the heavy oil asset, but in not charging him a fee for it.

As it turned out, oil prices stayed flat for the next three months, as did the capital markets, and the director couldn't complete the purchase. We were lucky. Within two years, oil had leaped in price, and the asset in question became worth well over $500 million. We nearly allowed someone to lift a valuable property while having no skin in the game—no risk. Real estate is not a sector in which I've ever had any interest or special knowledge. But it does appear to me that a lot of the activity in that business involves trying to scrounge free options to buy properties. Those options should be sold for five to ten percent of the property's value.

A free option is a terrible thing to give up, but a wonderful thing to own. One of the best examples of a free option that turned into a bonanza came from the world of sports. In the late 1960s, a group of entrepreneurs decided to start a new professional basketball league, the American Basketball Association. The league was a financial failure and, in 1976, it folded. Four of its teams were absorbed into the existing National Basketball Association (NBA).

Under the terms of the merger, those four clubs had to compensate the owners of the other, now-defunct ABA franchises. Rather than accepting just cash, the owners of the St. Louis franchise asked for something extra. They wanted, and got, the right to receive a portion of the survivors' television revenue "in perpetuity"—in effect, a free option on the future success of basketball broadcasts in the United States. For the three businessmen who'd owned the St. Louis team, it's estimated the deal has brought in well more than US$100 million to date.*

* The agreement made the list of The Dumbest Moments in Business History, compiled by *Business 2.0* magazine.

CHAPTER 19

DON'T LET CASH BURN A HOLE IN YOUR POCKET

Lowell, Massachusetts, was a depressed mill town when Dr. An Wang came along as its saviour. His company, Wang Laboratories, erected a massive headquarters there in the 1980s, with three twelve-storey towers, two smaller buildings, an auditorium, and parking for six hundred cars, all at enormous cost—between $50 and $60 million.

But Wang failed to keep up with the new era of cheap personal computers, and in 1992 the company filed for Chapter 11 bankruptcy protection. In 1994, shortly after it came out of restructuring, Wang decided to sell the Lowell campus. A local accountant bought it at the auction for $525,000—one cent for every dollar that was spent to build it.

It's amazing how cheap assets can become in a fire sale, and how far their values can fall. During the Japanese real estate bubble of the late 1980s and early 1990s, the land under Tokyo's Imperial Palace was said to be worth more than all the land in Florida. The average price of a 750-square-foot condominium in Tokyo rose to 70 million yen—about US$700,000, using 2006 exchange rates. Then came the crash. Many of those who bought into the hype own properties that are worth much less than they paid for them fifteen years ago.

Never let cash burn a hole in your pocket. Don't pay excessively for anything—a house, a stock, a piece of land—just because you have the money and the popular wisdom is that it can only get more expensive. (The popular view, remember, is often wrong!) The biggest opportunities come to those who can write a cheque when assets go on sale at knockdown prices—often during a period of economic turmoil or recession. Warren Buffett closed down a successful investment partnership in 1969 and liquidated most of its holdings, stuffing a lot of his own money into municipal bonds, because he felt that US equities were so richly valued they no longer made sense. He turned out to be right, and when the market plunged from 1972 to 1974, Buffett had the cash to make the investments that set him on the road to his fortune.

"Pay closer attention to where our revenue goes."

CHAPTER 20

TRACK THE CASH

In the summer of 1958, I was working as an assistant cutter in my father's housecoat factory. This was a small partnership called Diamond Tea Gown. The Viyella housecoats retailed for about $19.95 and sold in the top Canadian retail outlets.

Now, my father was about sixty years old and had evolved from a proficient dress designer into the chief operating officer and 50 per cent partner in this seventy-five-person manufacturing operation. His partner covered sales while my father handled design, textile procurement, and production.

At the end of a sultry summer day, I posed the following question to him: "Dad, you had no formal business training (unlike your know-it-all son), how do you monitor the business from a financial standpoint?"

His answer was splendidly simple. "I get a statement of the cash on hand every two weeks. If it's rising, I don't worry. If it's falling, I get concerned."

Now, the years went by and the son (me) went on to obtain a B.Sc. (chemistry and economics), an MBA (specializing in finance), and a CFA designation (chartered financial analyst). No metric that I ever encountered surpassed the simple wisdom of my non-financially educated father.

In every company in which I was a principal or an investor, the first metric tracked was always the level of cash. If the cash was rising, it meant several very positive things. Namely, the receivables were being collected, not too much buildup in the inventories was occurring, and, most important, the business was generating free cash flow.

In some businesses where optionality was being sold to investors, the cash rose due to recurring common share issues. To this day, I am provided a monthly cash sheet, two days after month end, for all my companies.

Now, if you're an engineer or medical doctor and get involved in managing a professional business or practice, the most important single thing to monitor is the trend of the cash levels in your enterprise.

On that summer day long ago, my very street-smart father imparted to me the metric that I've used my whole life to monitor the firms and partnerships where we had a stake: "Always track the cash levels."

"I'd like to introduce the advisor who convinced us
to invest in all those dot coms."

CHAPTER 21

INVESTORS' PERCEPTIONS OF RISKS ARE OVERINFLUENCED BY RECENT HISTORY (AMOS TVERSKY), OR, WHY FINANCIAL HISTORY IS SO IMPORTANT TO STUDY

It was called "Exchange Alley," and every day hordes of people gathered there to watch stock prices move, to trade, and to speculate. Grown men and women handed over their money to worthless companies, start-ups with fantasy business plans, and outright frauds. One company was raising money to build a perpetual motion machine; another planned to carry on "an undertaking of great advantage"—but nobody knew what it was.

It sounds like the dot-com delirium, circa 1999; in fact, what I've described is the madness that erupted

during Britain's South Sea equity bubble in 1720.*
Since the invention of the modern corporation more
than three hundred years ago, the world has wit-
nessed dozens of financial manias—a railway bubble
in the 1840s, mass speculation in stocks in the late
1920s, the so-called Nifty Fifty of the 1970s, the
Japanese bubble in the 1980s, and so on. Each one
ended in tears.

Financial history keeps repeating itself—that's why
it's among the most important subjects for any aspiring businessperson or investor to study. I'd say it's
almost as critical as accounting, which is the language
of business, and statistics, which teaches you to analyze probabilities and risks. You can't tell where we're
going unless you understand where we've been.

There's a very accurate saying about risk, one
that's been attributed to economist James Grant: Risk
is most threatening when it's least obvious, and least
threatening when it's most obvious. It's human nature
to extrapolate current trends far into the future, to
assume that excellent gains in the stock market (or
any financial market, including real estate) fore-
shadow even greater wealth to come. Investors are
too influenced by recent history. In reality, the reverse

* An excellent source on early financial bubbles, including the South
Sea bubble and the Dutch tulip craze, is Charles Mackay's classic
Extraordinary Popular Delusions and the Madness of Crowds.

is true—very high returns in the market usually produce inflated asset prices, which return to normal only after a long period of poor returns.

The best years or decades in the market usually began when stocks were irrationally cheap. Immediately after World War I, for example, investors could buy a dollar of profits from many US companies for $6 or $7 (that is, a price-earnings ratio of six or seven.) The low valuations were the fuel that helped ignite a stock market rally that ended only when prices appreciated too far; then came the Great Crash of 1929.

So what does history tell us about today? Over the past century, investors were willing to pay about $12 for every dollar of stock market earnings. Today, investors pay about $20 for dollar of earnings on the S&P 500 group of stocks, the largest American companies. Investors are paying too much for shares, based on the long-term record. But you have to be a student of financial history to understand this.

CHAPTER 22

CHINA

Every so often, something comes along—an event, a movement, a shift—that is so large, it reshapes the global economy and the fate of those who work in it. For your generation, that something is China.

In a book of this length, I can't make you an expert in China—no book can. It is too vast, too diverse, and changing too quickly. Nor can I say exactly how its industrialization will affect your life and your chosen career. But I am certain that what's happening there and in India will impact all of us for the next fifty years. Think about this: Philadelphia is America's fifth-largest city, with one and a half million people. The migration of Chinese peasants creates a new city or suburb the size of Philadelphia every month. There has never been anything like it in history. By transforming itself, China will transform the world.

What makes it so influential is not simply that it's the most populous nation on earth, with 1.3 billion people, or that it's a huge source of cheap labour, but that it is so open to trade and capital. For China, imports and exports represent a much larger proportion of the economic activity than for the United States, Japan, Brazil, or Europe, which consume more of their own output. In other words: China may not be the biggest economy on the planet (yet), but it's arguably the most important *trading* nation. If you want to prosper in the twenty-first century, you'll need to understand it.

The best way is to visit it. I did in 2005, and it was one of the most important and rewarding trips I've ever taken. What follows are some of my observations and conclusions from that journey.

I prepared for the trip by reading Ted C. Fishman's excellent book, *China Inc.* Fishman, a writer and former trader who spent two years in China, made these points:

1. Three hundred million rural Chinese will move to cities in the next fifteen years.

2. General Motors expects the Chinese automobile market to be bigger than the US market by 2025. Some seventy-four million Chinese families can now afford to buy cars.

3. China has more speakers of English as a second language than America has native English speakers, and more Internet users than the United States. It has 320 million people under the age of fourteen—more than the entire US population.

4. China has more than three hundred biotech firms that operate unhindered by animal rights lobbies, religious groups, or ethical standards boards.

5. On average, American companies make a 42 per cent return on their China operations.

6. Apparel workers in the United States make $9.56 an hour. In El Salvador, they make $1.65. In China they make between 68¢ and 88¢.

7. There are 186 MBA programs in China.

THOUGHTS AND OBSERVATIONS FROM BEIJING

There are more than two thousand buildings under construction in the Chinese capital. Developers have free rein to raze old neighbourhoods and relocate elderly residents to the suburbs. Many of the new buildings are government offices.

One family in three owns a car. Traffic is fierce, but the road system is extensive and in excellent condition. There are lots of toll roads. China's Communist government has no aversion to letting private investors build infrastructure. (Compare this to Ontario, where the privatization of a single toll highway, the 407, causes years of controversy.) I went sixty miles to Dalian, China's third-largest port. The road was four lanes and excellent the entire route.

My impression of Beijing and Shanghai is that China has the most disciplined population I've ever seen outside of Switzerland. The hotel staff were young, motivated, and professional. The hotels were as good as any I've seen in the world. There was no graffiti, and all the streets and parks were immaculate (much cleaner than in Toronto).

The policy of only one child per family is very real. It is enforced and, amazingly, appears to have acceptance.

While wages of US$150 per month (versus Hong Kong's US$1,300 per month) are very low by our standards, there are winners emerging everywhere in their economy. The lack of religion and churches does not appear to be missed by the Chinese I spoke with. It frees up the population to concentrate on their economic condition.

In Beijing, I had dinner in The Great Hall of the People. It was the best dinner venue I've seen in my life, with sixty-foot ceilings and more marble than in any Italian church. Tiananmen Square and the Summer Palace were both very exciting visiting sites. The Great Wall of China and the Forbidden City would both make my list of the top ten lifetime touring highlights. Overall, Beijing is in a class of its own as a tourist destination.

SHANGHAI — THE BUSINESS CAPITAL OF CHINA

There are more than three hundred buildings higher than fifteen storeys under construction in Shanghai. To accomplish this degree of development, more than eight hundred thousand houses have been demolished, and one million people have moved to high-rise apartments in the suburbs. There are more than five thousand high-rise buildings in Shanghai. Skyscraper building in this city is the equivalent of building the entire city of Manhattan each and every year.

The city has a long-term plan in place for the next hundred years. The airport is two miles long and served by a magnetic-levitation train (running at 460 kilometres per hour [280 miles per hour]), which goes downtown in six minutes. (Again, compare this to Toronto, where almost no new transit infrastructure has been built in the past twenty years, there's no rail connection from the airport to downtown, and no redevelopment of the downtown waterfront.)

While the infrastructure is quite good, energy is a problem. Coal-burning power stations create pollution problems in both cities I visited.

English was the second language everywhere I went in China. If you want to learn another language, I'd suggest Mandarin.

HONG KONG (7.5 MILLION PEOPLE)

This city reminds me of Montreal in 1977, just as Toronto was assuming the mantle of Canada's business capital. It is run by old establishment families who, in time, will be overrun by the meritocracy arising in Shanghai and the rest of China. A 4,000-square-foot apartment here costs US$8 million. This city has nowhere to go or grow. The twenty-first century will not belong to Hong Kong, in my opinion.

KEEPING UP ON CHINA FROM AFAR

A great website to track is www.chinadaily.com.cn, put out by the major Chinese newspaper in English. Go to this site and click on the business page. It's a great window on events in China. In two weeks of reading *China Daily*, I gleaned the following facts:

- China will build forty nuclear reactors over the next fifteen years. This only increases its proportion of electricity generated by nuclear power from 2.4 per cent to 4 per cent. The average among countries with nuclear power plants is 17 per cent.

- By 2020, autos on China's roads are expected to swell to one hundred million, from twenty-four million today.

- Coal supplies 70 per cent of China's energy needs.

- The market for diamond jewellery is about US$1.2 billion in China today. China is the fifth-largest national consumer of diamonds in the world. The luxury-goods market in China is 11 per cent of the global total.

- Twenty million square metres of new apartment space were completed in Shanghai in 2004.

- There are currently 6,300 active construction sites occupying sixty-two million square metres in Beijing.

CONCLUDING THOUGHTS ABOUT CHINA

The Chinese people are disciplined, smart, and motivated. They have a vision and are determined to realize it. They will, over the next fifty years, remake themselves from a nation of subsistence farmers and peasants to a modern, dynamic economy with a sizable middle class.

This trend is real and will last far longer than most financial pundits visualize. Those who can figure out how to supply China with what it needs—whether it's oil, commodities, gold, or financial expertise—and who invest to take advantage of its rapid development will prosper.

"I will now perform the delivery dance
of the flamboyant speaker."

CHAPTER 23

SPEECHES—TEN RULES TO UTILIZE

Over a span of forty years, I have given a few hundred speeches. Here are some key rules I've acquired:

1. *Be brief:*
   People's attention span is limited. Nobody ever complained about a speech being too short! Tell your audience right up front how long the speech is going to run. This signals how long they'll have to pay attention.

2. *Try to communicate one main idea:*
   A common mistake is trying to pack into a speech four or five ideas. People are likely to remember only one idea, theme, or concept.

In a lecture to students, the same principles apply. Leave a lot of time for questions. Use audio-visual aids that are funny and attention-getting.

3. *Create a surprise:*

    People love to be surprised. As I got older, I always used the concept of surprise. Examples are:

    (A) having your entrance and exit marked by exciting folk songs or music;

    (B) saying something like, "This a serious speech—above all there will be no clowning around." Then have twelve clowns enter the room, making noise, handing out cards, and leaving in ninety seconds;

    (C) instead of clowns, have a group of cheerleaders burst in and lead a cheer for an honoured guest.

4. *Use humour:*

    Collect joke books and select three or four good one-liners or zingers. Comedy is very hard to do well. Test your material on several people in advance. Personalize jokes by inserting the names of prominent people in the audience into the comedy material. This creates a sense of participation and identification by the audience.

5. *Slow it down:*
   Talk slowly and mark lots of points to pause. Give the audience time to comprehend and assimilate your messages. There's nothing worse than a speaker who rushes through a script he reads.

6. *Use cue cards and look up often:*
   Don't appear to read your material. Make protracted eye contact with your audience. Talk with them, don't read to them.

7. *Self-praise is no honour:*
   Get a good two-minute lead-in from someone who tells your audience why you're very important and why they should listen to you.

8. *Never speak before the main course in a dinner speech:*
   Don't get between people and their food. (The same principle applies to dogs.)

9. *Reuse good material:*
   Write a good speech then keep finding new audiences on which to utilize all or parts of it.

10. *Use positive body language:*
   Smile, and use your hands to make and emphasize points. Get out from behind the podium if possible.

"How would you describe my leadership?
Great, greater or greatest?"

CHAPTER 24

WHAT IS A LEADER?

Asked once by a journalist to recall the best piece of advice he'd ever received, Andrew Grove, the man who built Intel Corp., quoted the words of an old college professor: "When 'everybody knows' that something is so, nobody knows nothin'."

Grove is living proof of this. The invention that made Intel and launched the digital age—a microprocessor so tiny it can fit on your fingernail, yet do thousands of calculations every second—was something once thought by physicists to be impossible. "Everybody knew" that it couldn't be done. In proving the experts wrong, Grove and his partners displayed the qualities I think are most important in any leader: persistence, discipline, conviction, judgment, and an ability to share the credit.

Persistence and patience are key ideas I've discussed elsewhere in this book. You won't get anywhere without them. But discipline is important, too—probably more now than ever in the age of e-mail, BlackBerry pagers, the Internet, and constant distraction. What do I mean by discipline? To me it's simple: it's the ability to figure out what's worth your time and effort, what's not, and to cut out the latter.

This is a skill you can acquire—indeed, it's one that I think almost all successful people in business, politics, or academia *must* acquire. For a time in the 1980s, I was managing billions of dollars for pension funds, running a growing mining company with Pierre Lassonde, investing in start-up companies through our merchant bank, and raising two daughters with my wife. I was busy. One of the hazards of working in finance is that people always want a piece of your time; a money manager could spend twenty-four hours every day with analysts or salespeople from the investment dealers.

But I eventually figured out how to get them out of my office—and my day—so I could concentrate on the more important things. Most achievers have this trait of being able to filter out the demands on their time. PIMCO's Bill Gross is one of the world's most influential investors in bonds, yet he doesn't carry a BlackBerry, doesn't answer any emails he doesn't want to, and doesn't spend much time on the phone, because he believes his time is better spent on reading and analyzing. An old expression goes, "Givers have to set limits because takers never do." That applies to your time and energy.

Persistence and discipline can be learned. The third and fourth traits—conviction and good judgment— are innate, in my opinion. You either have them or you don't. To have conviction—to hold steady to a belief that what "everybody knows" is wrong—is not easy. Humans seem to have a herding instinct that makes them want to coalesce around popular or widely held ideas and theories. But when I think about the biggest mistakes I've made, they were usually when I did something because everyone else was doing it. And many of the best decisions were in defiance of the conventional wisdom of the day (investing in oil sands properties in Northern Alberta when few analysts believed the price of oil could go higher than $35 a barrel, for example). Conviction and good judgment go hand in hand. Standing against the tide of opinion won't do you much good if you have your facts or your reasoning wrong.

Finally, a true leader shares the rewards of success. Quite a few years ago, I had the occasion to visit

Sweden. While touring one of the main museums in Stockholm, which featured the country's Viking heritage, I came across the following inscription:

> In the Viking Age—800 AD to 1100 AD—the power of a ruler depended in large measure on his ability to reward his followers.
>
> —P.H. Sawyer, *Kings and Vikings*

After a career spanning forty-three years, nothing I have seen on the subject of leadership has been more astute. I had the message made into cards and have handed out hundreds to CEOs and aspiring leaders.

"Every time I come up with a great idea, you have to bring up the law and prison."

CHAPTER 25

PARTNERS

Many of the greatest start-ups in the past thirty years began as teams of two. Examples: Berkshire, Apple, Oracle, Cisco, Yahoo, and Google.

Good partners are a blessing! All my life, I've worked with partners. They have all been of enormous help in running and selling the businesses in which we were involved. In addition, my life partner has been of incomparable help in rearing our children. (In the long run, this task is more important than any business.)

The primary benefit of partners is as a sounding board. Many times the super idea or concept has arrived in my head (usually at night). This flash of insight was usually so profound I could hardly wait to get to work and disclose the epiphany to my long-suffering partners. Often, upon being presented with the idea, my partners would patiently point out that although the idea was superficially interesting, I had forgotten to consider four or five factors, which turned the idea into a mere mind fart.

The other area in which partners have excelled is widening my skill sets or specializations and filling in when I was sick or dealing with a family crisis. One of my partners endured a terrible twelve-month ordeal of losing his wife to cancer. The task of running two public companies fell on me and two or three colleagues. It's important in an owner-operated company to have very committed colleagues to fill the voids created by failing health that the journey through life often deals to us.

THE GOLDEN RULE OF PARTNERSHIP

The key to a successful partnership is mutual veto power. If you cannot agree on a major proposition, you don't do it.

The key partners in my life were: Tanna Schulich (thirty-six years); Pierre Lassonde (twenty-three years); Austin Beutel (twenty-two years); Ned Goodman (fifteen years); Ann Brown (twenty-eight years); and David Williams (twenty years).

Other folks who played partner-type roles included: Craig Haase (nineteen years); Owen McCreery (twenty years); David Harquail (fifteen years); Ron Binns (sixteen years); and Sharon Dowdall (ten years).

AN OLD CHINESE PROVERB

Behind an able man, there are always other able men! (This was always the case with us.)

GREAT PARTNERS

Qualities of such people are loyalty, respect, enthusiasm, and being team players.

From a speech by Jack Welch, CEO of General Electric, upon his retirement:

> Together, we've all done things we never imagined. We've all gone places we never thought we would see. We've all reached dreams we never thought possible. I came from a place just like most of you, and I got lucky thanks to all of your good work. Thanks for being so special. I love you all.

A POEM FOR EGOMANIACS:

The Indispensable Man

Sometime when you're feeling important,
Sometime when your ego's in bloom,
Sometime when you take it for granted,
You're the best qualified in the room.

Take a bucket and fill it with water,
Put your hand in it up to the wrist,
Pull it out and the hole that's remaining,
Is the measure of how you'll be missed.

—Saxon White Kessinger

"I'm on my way to tell the CEO he's dead wrong about everything.
Who wants to come with me?"

CHAPTER 26

DEALING WITH BOSSES OR SUCCESSFUL PEOPLE

There's a great story about a pompous businessman with a boundless ego going up to a famous northern Canadian fishing camp. This fellow fancied himself a world-class fisherman. He was a legend in his own mind. His Greenheart rods and Bogden reels, which had price tags as big as his ego, reinforced his self-esteem.

He hired the best guide available and told him, "Look boy—take me to the pool with the biggest fish." They hiked through the bog for forty minutes until they came to a clear pool full of gigantic Arctic char.

The guide went to sleep with his back leaning on a tree. Mr. Big unfurled his $20,000 worth of gear and started casting. An hour went by and, despite dropping flies in front of countless huge fish, none of them took the bait.

Mr. Big marched up to the old guide, kicked him in the foot to awaken him, and said, "These damn fish won't bite." The guide slowly awakened and said to Mr. Big, "They didn't get big by being stupid."

Not a bad thing to remember when dealing with a boss whose decisions you don't quite understand. It's also helpful to be able to recognize—and adapt to—the styles of people you work for and with. I once went to a seminar on this topic at which the speaker said any group of employees can be divided into four groups: amiables, drivers, analytics, and dreamers.

Amiables, as the word suggests, want to be liked. They're good listeners and team players. They're responsive. But they can also be indecisive, and they are usually reluctant to get rid of malcontents or other toxic people.

Drivers are the tough guys. They rise early, work long hours, make decisions quickly, and demand a lot of themselves and others. Working for them can be difficult, but—if you can get along with them—very rewarding. Drivers make the best CEOs.

Analytics are the deep thinkers. They're the ones who will lock themselves in a room to assess all the facts. When they make decisions, they are more systematic about it than drivers. Sometimes, they can seem emotionally distant—don't expect a lot of small talk from a boss who's an analytic.

Dreamers are just that—people with a lot of pie-in-the-sky ideas who leave it to others to worry about the details of their high-concept plans. While they can have their role in a company, they are usually far too indecisive to take on leadership roles. I've seen dreamers wreak havoc in companies. My advice is to stay away from them as much as you can.

This theory of working styles was developed by two American management consultants, Robert Bolton and Dorothy Grover Bolton. Their view was that if we understand our own styles and those of the people we work with, teamwork becomes easier, and I think there's a lot of truth in that.

"Today's talk will be about the dangers of mobile computing while standing under a tree during a thunderstorm."

CHAPTER 27

THE MEDIA, YOUR LIFE, AND STATISTICAL ODDS

In the spring of 2003, the city of Toronto was hit with an outbreak of a strange, highly contagious pneumonia known as severe acute respiratory syndrome. The SARS epidemic, as it became known in the media, gave the city international attention of the most unflattering kind.

When the World Health Organization issued an advisory against travelling to Toronto, the reaction was panic. Two children's choirs from the United States cancelled their plans to come to the city for a festival. The Toronto Blue Jays baseball team received twenty thousand cancelled orders for tickets. Top executives from an international film-theatre company refused to come to the city for a scheduled annual meeting, instead broadcasting their speeches from New York via satellite. Conventions were called off. Tourists stayed away, and many of those who didn't wore surgical masks as they disembarked at Pearson International Airport. The hysteria was far-reaching: Even the Anne of Green Gables museum in Prince Edward Island, a popular spot for Japanese tourists, saw a temporary decline in visitors, though the island had no cases of SARS and is thousands of miles from Toronto!

What were the odds of catching SARS in Toronto that spring? Jeffrey Rosenthal, a professor of statistics at the University of Toronto, gives us the numbers:

Number of deaths due to SARS in Toronto in 2003:
fewer than 50.
Number of deaths in Canada from the common flu
in a typical year: 1,000.

"A traveller visiting Toronto, even at the height of the SARS outbreak, was about as likely to die of influenza as of SARS," Rosenthal writes in his book *Struck by Lightning: The Curious World of Probabilities*, "but I cannot recall any front-page headlines about an influenza outbreak, nor do I know of any tourists who changed their travel plans or behaviour patterns to avoid contracting influenza."

I knew an old, successful Nevada mining promoter who never read newspapers. He claimed he
couldn't remain optimistic if he was inundated daily
with a barrage of bad news. The media focus on aber-
rations—that's what "news" is. If five million people
live in a relatively safe urban area like Toronto, and
five of them are murdered in a single week, you are
likely to see and hear about a wave of violent crime
overtaking the city. Good news doesn't sell. No one
buys a newspaper or listens to the radio or watches
television to hear that a thousand planes landed
safely, or that the police handled no unusual acts of
crime, or that nothing particularly eventful happened
that day.

To keep a positive outlook, you need to keep perspective. Don't allow the media to infect you with a
negative view or a sense of helplessness about the
world's many social and economic problems. Try to
skim the bad news in newspapers and focus on
broader economic and social trends.

A little knowledge of statistical odds can help.
Many people have a fear of flying; perhaps they
wouldn't if they knew the odds of dying in a plane
crash are at least one in two million, according to
Rosenthal. The well-documented fact that flying is
safer than highway travel does not give the least bit of
comfort to the female members of my family, none of

whom seem to have acquired the gene for understanding the probabilities of disaster.

In a quarter-century of hiking, despite odds of millions to one, I have had to endure countless warnings from my beloved wife about impending doom from bears (two seen in twenty-five years), snakes (also two in twenty-five years), tarantulas (none), cougars (I've never seen one), and, of course, lightning. The biggest hiking danger came from a bad case of tendonitis brought on by a mad 2,500-foot descent in a thundershower near Crested Butte, Colorado. My wife beat me down that mountain by a good thirty minutes.

She didn't realize that the odds of being hit by lightning are infinitesimally small; only three people in Canada were killed by lightning in 2000. A Canadian is far more likely to die in a fire or from accidental poisoning—but even those are extraordinarily rare events. Most deaths in North America are caused by one of two things: heart disease or cancer. Rosenthal writes: "It makes far more sense to take care of your health than it does to worry about being murdered—to say nothing of deaths from terrorism, airplane crashes, drowning, burning or lightning." As for the threat of SARS: In 2005, the World Health Organization declared the disease eradicated.

"No, we don't know what happened to all your money.
Is it important?"

CHAPTER 28

INVESTING IN FOREIGN COUNTRIES

One of Canada's most successful entrepreneurs, Jim Pattison, said: "You can probably know a maximum of three countries well enough to successfully invest in." Personally, I'd restrict myself to one or two. Roger Rosenblatt's *Rules for Aging* (see Chapter 8) says that if you want to live a long time, avoid swinish people. I'd expand this to include swinish countries where the rule of law is absent, property rights are questionable, and governments expropriate without compensation.

My view on this stems from personal, sometimes unpleasant, experience. The chief characteristic of a swinish country is that it is governed by people who have little sense of how to create wealth but no shortage of imagination when it comes to stealing it. They'll change laws with no warning, concoct phony tax assessments, or alter the contracts under which foreign companies operate. I was an investor in a private energy venture that owned natural gas rights in Ukraine. The government there allowed us to bring the gas to within one hundred yards of the border, then simply took it to prevent us from exporting at much higher prices. Another company I've been involved with, this one in mining, was forced to sell an asset for $40 million less than it was worth. The buyers? Friends of the local governing party. Canada's role in bringing an end to apartheid in South Africa earned no points for Franco-Nevada when we wanted to merge with Johannesburg-based Gold Fields in 2000. The ANC government there strung us along for more than a year and never did give its consent.

I've personally had or watched colleagues suffer through very unhappy investing experiences in Indonesia, Mexico, England's North Sea, China, and Venezuela. The US has much stronger property rights than any of those countries—yet it, too, can be a minefield because of the power of the tort lawyers. Even in Canada, all provinces do not have equally friendly attitudes toward outside investors; Newfoundland and British Columbia tend to be the worst.

You can usually find enough business opportunities in more hospitable places.

"Oh, you wanted to enjoy your computer.
That will cost another $400."

CHAPTER 29

SPENDING MONEY

My father told me as a young boy, "You must make enough in your chosen profession to afford to be screwed by every other profession or vendor of consumer goods, because you will be."

For a long time, I thought this was an uncharacteristically negative view of life. With age has come the realization that this warning was pretty accurate.

I recently bought ties in China for $1.25 each, which compare favourably to $100 Italian ties, $150 Swiss ties, and $225 British ties. It looks like I've paid too much for ties most of my life.

If you think Daddy's warning is too cynical, try going to the average garage to get your car repaired.

My father had a golden rule regarding the spending of money. He always said, "When the money is in your pocket, you're the boss. Once it's transferred to the merchant, he's in charge."

Another approach Dad prescribed is: see if you still want the item in question twenty-four or forty-eight hours later. It's amazing how often a cooling-off period kills the ardour of a purchaser.

In the purchase of private companies, old-timers like my dad always held back part of the purchase price conditional on the collection of receivables, the possible emergence of unrecorded liabilities, and undisclosed problems with the inventory.

Contractors (especially when conditions are booming) love to get a big deposit (say, 50 per cent). And when they do, they have you hostage. This ties you up to them. They then show up intermittently as they juggle several jobs.

Getting a square deal with contractors is an art form best left to professionals such as builders or architects.

CHAPTER 30

THE OIL INDUSTRY

It's a myth that I made the bulk of my money in the gold industry. The bulk of my estate derived from the oil industry. Since 1965 (when I was twenty-five), for more than forty years, I have been involved with fifteen oil companies as a principal, investor, or director (see Appendix III).

Most of the activity was centred in Calgary, which I first visited in 1965. At that time, the city numbered about three hundred thousand inhabitants and had only two buildings of eight storeys in height. One connector has been my old friend Alvin Libin, a real estate/nursing home financier, whose positive attitude and local knowledge I've enjoyed for more than forty years.

I did have companies that ventured into the US with bases in Houston and Dallas. Most Canadian junior oil firms have done poorly in the US. I've had two huge wins and one failure down south. My advice is stick to companies that invest and operate in Canada.

I had a small investment in Ukraine. I watched people and careers destroyed by sheer brazen theft and expropriation without compensation. Some folks might make money in foreign oil plays. My advice is avoid them like the very plague itself.

Historically, oil has better profit margins than mining and is an industry more than ten times the size of mining. Oil's and mining's great attraction is that you can double or triple the size (value) of a company with one drill hole. No other industry can create wealth as rapidly.

Oil is entering a golden age of shortage of supply. Very tight oil markets will last for the next thirty to fifty years, until fusion power becomes commercialized. Fusion power will drive all cars electrically and power all homes. Oil may still be used for chemicals and flying planes. Its age will end as did the ages of wood power and coal power.

"Don't worry. We paid a consultant a lot of money
to tell us we're going the right way."

CHAPTER 31

BUSINESS AXIOMS

(A) Business is a means to an end not an end in itself. Nobody on his or her deathbed says, "I wish I had spent more time in the office."

(B) Never quit a job unless you have another job. My father taught me this great truth. You are perceived as more valuable if you are working than if you're unemployed. You may feel staying employed doesn't give you the time or latitude to seek a better job. This is a dangerous delusion—don't succumb to it.

(C) Always ask the question "If this decision is wrong, is it going to be painful or fatal?" Company builders and business leaders keep away from "bet the company" investments.

(D) Keep away from advisors/consultants. If they knew how to make money, they would. These folks are like the fellow who knows a thousand ways to make love but doesn't know any women.

(E) The best test of a deal's true attraction is to ask your partners, employees, directors, family, and so on, "Would you put your own money in this deal?" It's amazing how often the answer to this question is, "No! This is good for the company, but I'll take a pass." These deals are invariably losers.

(F) Always have at least two people from your side present at any negotiating or deal-making sessions. This gives you time to think, plus an ally with whom to compare perceptions.

(G) Never confront or threaten people or institutions who have more power than you. Examples: police, customs agents, the SEC, Ontario Securities Commission, tax agents of the government, or politicians.

(H) In dealing with the media, never forget to qualify your statements with "not for attribution" and "off the record" where appropriate. Journalists value their contacts and will usually respect a source's desires.

(I) In negotiations, always try to get the other party to name its asking price. It may often be far lower than your maximum offer. If the other party won't name a price, start very low. You can always go up.

(J) Almost everything in life is easier to get into than get out of.

(K) Never bid against yourself. Only raise your bid to top a real counter bid, not an imaginary one.

"I can't talk now. I'm discussing strategy
with our financial consultant."

CHAPTER 32

MONEY MANAGEMENT AND FINANCE AS CAREERS

When I was young, money management and finance weren't the popular career choices they are now. Every year, thousands of new graduates are drawn to work on Bay Street and Wall Street, where the hours are long—especially in investment banking—but the opportunity exists for very high pay. The field of financial services has grown into one of North America's most profitable industries. In 1960, you'd have found very few securities firms among the world's largest companies. In 2006, seven of them made the Fortune 500.

A great way for young folks to understand the attraction of these fields is to read *The (Practical) Guide to Finding the (Right) Finance Jobs in Canada* by David

Price. This book reviews nine areas of finance and contains profiles of veterans and newcomers who work on the Street; it outlines a typical working day and describes the personality traits you need to work in finance. It's a good starting point.

My personal experience is as follows:

I worked as a security analyst for a small brokerage firm, Eastern Securities, from 1966 to 1969. My boss was a superb salesman named Bob Stewart (he remains a friend to this day). In 1969, I became a chartered financial analyst (CFA), the 2,369th person to get that professional designation. Today, there are about 70,000 CFAs around the world.

For the next twenty-two years, until 1990, I worked in investment management as a partner with Austin Beutel, Ned Goodman, David Williams, and Owen McCreery. In my career at Beutel, Goodman and Co., I ran mutual funds, pension funds, and private accounts, and was an oil industry analyst. I also did venture capital investing and merchant banking for a series of small, exploratory oil and mining companies.

By the time I was in my early thirties, I'd had exposure to several kinds of finance jobs, and I've spent the rest of my working life immersed in them or watching them up close. Here are a few observations about the profession that was the springboard for my business career:

(A) I began in a time before the explosion of derivative products, which have complicated the investment world and enriched stockbrokers. In my CFA studies of the late 1960s, there was hardly any material on derivatives. Today the subject consumes entire textbooks.

Derivatives trading may be a good career choice for those who are mathematically brilliant. But it's perilous for anyone else because it's a zero-sum game—with derivatives, one man's profit is always another's loss. (I don't believe, for example, that the finance professionals who work at hedging commodities for mining or oil companies can prevail against the banks who are taking the other side of the trade. The banks can devote much more human and intellectual capital to the job.)

(B) Sell-side analysis, despite excellent pay and a high profile, isn't what it used to be. Research departments have sold out to investment banking as the economics of the brokerage business have evolved. It's much harder to make money now from trading commissions, and the big profits are earned from underwriting. I don't believe that's about to change, despite the Wall Street research scandal at the start of this decade, where the biggest US securities firms paid hundreds of millions of dollars to settle charges that they published misleading reports that favoured corporate clients.

Even in firms where analysts have retained their independence, they are overworked. They cover too many securities in too little time and are required to make judgments too quickly—with the result that their analysis is, in many cases, useless. I was recently the largest stockholder in a small, oil producing company. Seven analysts followed the stock and thought it was worth between $6 and $17 a share—the average was $12.50. The company was bought out by a major integrated oil company for $24 a share. Where was the analytical competence of the sell-side analysts?

(C) Buy-side analysts, who work for mutual fund, pension fund, or private investment managers, have more time to investigate ideas. But their judgment is held up to the ruthless scrutiny of performance reviews by outside consultants. If there's a downside to the investment management business, it's that it operates under a giant contradiction: It takes five to ten years to build a good firm and a track record, and clients often say they're interested only in long-term results—yet performance is rated quarterly.

To illustrate this, I've often given the real-life example of an oil stock I invested in and held for five years. For the first four years it traded between $10 and $15 per share. In the fifth year it rose to $150 per share. Now, for the first four years, the consultants would have given me poor ratings. In the fifth year, I became a genius!

As stupid as the consulting system is, it is, unfortunately, a fixture in some parts of the money management business, particularly pension funds. Only people like Warren Buffett, some hedge funds, and rich old–money managers like me have the luxury of telling the performance consultants to piss off. Until recently, I had 72 per cent of my net worth in three stocks (one was subsequently bought out for nearly seven times my purchase price). There's not a consultant in the world who would condone such irresponsible behaviour. But then, not many consultants are very rich.

(D) The most rewarding part of the finance profession is merchant banking, in my opinion. This consists of investing in start-up or small companies, going on the board, and helping build a successful enterprise over five to ten years. My partners Ned Goodman, Austin Beutel, and Pierre Lassonde have each done this numerous times in their careers. They're masters of the game of company creation.

My merchant banking activity has created enormous employment and economic benefits to Canada, and great wealth and personal satisfaction for my co-investors, managements, and myself. Merchant banking is where I earned the capital to pursue my philanthropic objectives, secured my family's welfare, and attained many of my life's goals.

Here's a little poem I would like to dedicate to all the wonderful promoters and stockbrokers I have ever known:

> Alas! I'm tied to Wall Street where
> They reckon me a millionaire,
> And sometimes in a day alone
> I gain a fortune o'er the phone.
> Yet I to be a man was made,
> And here I ply this sorry trade
> Of Company manipulation,
> Of selling short and stock inflation:
> I whom God meant to rope a steer,
> Fate made a Wall Street buccaneer.

> —*Robert Service*

"I hope you'll appreciate the elegant nuance in the way I say no."

CHAPTER 33

A SUCCESSFUL BUSINESSPERSON HAS TO LEARN TO SAY NO!

"The art of leadership is saying no, not yes. It is very easy to say yes." Tony Blair was talking about governing when he said those words, but he could just as easily have been discussing one of the secrets of commerce.

This piece of wisdom was instilled in me many years ago by Joe Rotman, an entrepreneur who is the benefactor of the Rotman School of Business at the University of Toronto. Many years ago, prior to the philanthropic work that made him famous, I arranged for a meeting so that I could gather the insight of an astute businessman who'd built a fortune in the resource business, primarily through oil and gas production.

"Every successful businessperson has to learn how to say no," he told me that day. If you spend your life in business, you will see dozens or perhaps hundreds of potential deals. A small number will be highly attractive; most will be average or below average. The path to superior results is to accept only the best ideas—indeed, no venture capitalist or merchant banker could survive for very long without saying no to 90 per cent (or more) of the pitches he sees.

You can be diplomatic, firm, or a combination of the two, but you must be comfortable with the idea of handing out rejection. Rotman's lesson became rooted deeply in my consciousness and caused me to be much less wimpy about turning down venture capital deals, start-up companies, and charities.

"We're selling 100,000 shares in an idea we plan to have after raising enough capital to think about it."

CHAPTER 34

SKIN IN THE GAME

As a lad of twenty years old, I bought my first car for $700. It was a 1957 Ford Fairlane, red on the bottom with a gold swish bar separating a white top. To me, it was the most beautiful car in the whole world. Before this, I had always borrowed my dad's car to go out on Saturday night dates.

On a sunny Saturday morning, my father found me in the laneway of the apartment building where we lived, feverishly washing and waxing my new car. Then he asked one of the most thought-provoking questions of my life. Why, in the three years of driving it, had I never washed (let alone waxed) *his* car? The answer was simple: I had no pride of ownership in his car!

This was 1960, when the Cold War battle of capitalism versus Communism was at its height. My father said, "This feeling you have, son, is why Communism will fail." At the time, that was in considerable doubt, but I knew that my father had struck a note in me, and it lasts to this day. A human's attitude and behaviour change completely if he owns something, or has "skin in the game."

Compare home owners to renters in their care of the properties they live in. Look at people's behaviour in rental cars versus cars they own. Study businesses that have profit-sharing plans versus government bureaucracies. Government's record of managing is so poor because civil servants have no ownership or skin in the game.

The record of owner-operated companies is far superior to records of companies run by "professional" management. Many manager-operated companies attempt to create the feeling of ownership with stock options. But these are one-way motivators; there's not any financial pain inflicted by a failure. Stock options, performance fees (such as those paid to hedge funds), and other owner-simulation tools—which give managers the upside but none of the downside—often cause managers to embark on grand adventures with other people's money. Time Warner CEO Gerald Levin owned fewer than one million shares but held seven million stock options in early 2000, when he negotiated his company's union with America Online—one of the worst mergers in modern business history. I doubt he would have agreed to the deal if those numbers had been reversed!

When you're investing in stocks, your chances for success are greatly improved when you pick companies where the officers and directors own a large amount of stock. If you ran a list of the best long-term investments in Canada, you'd come up with names like Home Capital, CI Financial, Thomson, Franco-Nevada, and many other companies that are (or were) managed by people who owned a lot of shares.

In your career, you may at some point get the chance to put some skin in the game. Early in mine, I had the opportunity to take a high-paying job as an analyst in New York. At the same time, Ned Goodman and Austin Beutel recruited me to join their small investment firm at a much lower salary but with the chance to become an equal partner. To my father, it looked like an easy decision. I did go to Beutel Goodman and never regretted it. I don't think a person can ever get really rich working for someone else, although there are other forms of psychic and altruistic satisfaction in many career lines.

"I don't like that answer. Give our market advisor another spin."

CHAPTER 35

ON BUYING A BUSINESS (OR, BETTER YET, STARTING ONE)

William D. Smithburg is not a name that will show up on any list of the world's most accomplished businessmen. But he is famous all the same. In 1994, toward the end of a lengthy career as chairman and CEO of the Quaker Oats Company, Smithburg became the architect of one of the best-known deals of the decade when he decided that Quaker should buy the Snapple Beverage Company.

The Romans coined the expression "Caveat emptor"—let the buyer beware—because the seller always knows more than the buyer. Smithburg apparently hadn't studied his Latin. Snapple, which made beverages that were healthier than carbonated soft drinks, had grown quickly in the early 1990s, and he was so persuaded of the merits of owning it that he missed the signs of trouble. Snapple's business was under attack from competing products like Nestea and Lipton. Inventories of unsold drinks were building up. Smithburg knew about some of these problems before he made the deal, but others came as a surprise. The distributors who earned fat profit margins selling Snapple revolted against Quaker's attempts to save money by tinkering with that system. Even Snapple's manufacturing setup was a mess.*

My father once warned me, "Nobody sells a good, growing business." There are exceptions— sometimes owners sell when their health is poor and there's no one to take over the business—but for the most part, his advice is correct. You will usually create much more wealth by starting a new business than buying an existing one. Most of mine came from start-ups in investment management, oil and gas exploration, and mining royalties. Scan the list of Forbes billionaires, and you'll see dozens of people whose fortunes were created not by what they bought but what they built—Bill Gates, Michael Dell, the Walton family (Wal-Mart), the Johnson family (Fidelity mutual funds)—and those are just some of the famous ones.

* Quaker's follies are outlined in great detail in Robert F. Bruner's book *Deals from Hell*.

Remember: ability is the poor man's wealth. Don't pander to the establishment looking for a break; they didn't get where they are by giving things away or helping people like you. And if you are confronted with the chance to buy a business, collect as much intelligence as you can on the seller's motivation—it could save you a lot of grief. Ask William Smithburg: less than three years after buying Snapple for $1.7 billion, Quaker sold it for about $300 million, and he resigned.

"We dominated the market, and utterly destroyed our competition, but during our victory party we fell back to 120th place."

CHAPTER 36

DEALS AND INVESTMENTS

The five questions to ask when screening a potential deal or investment:

1. How much can I make?	• upside
2. How much can I lose?	• downside
3. How do I get my money back?	• liquidity
4. Who says this deal is any good?	• management record
5. Who else is in the deal?	• endorsement

The upside/downside equation:
If you walked into a Las Vegas casino and found a slot machine that gave you an even chance of winning, you'd consider yourself fortunate. But fifty-fifty or even sixty-forty propositions aren't anywhere near good enough in deal making and investing. Successful deal making requires only two things, really: an ability to assess odds, and the discipline to act only when the odds are heavily in your favour.

That's it.

Going against the crowd:
A great rule of markets, deal making, and life is: "When everybody thinks something is so, it usually isn't." Many of the best deals or investments are made by going against popular opinion (but only after you've done your homework). Warren Buffett made a killing buying GEICO, the US auto insurer, when others thought it was going broke. Fidelity fund manager Peter Lynch built a large stake in Chrysler starting in 1982. That year heralded one of the worst recessions of the twentieth century, and you couldn't have found a less popular investment at the time than a struggling American automaker—Chrysler had been rescued from the brink of bankruptcy by the US government only two years before. Yet it became one of Lynch's most profitable investments ever.

Oil stocks were unloved in 1998 when the price of crude oil sank to $11 a barrel. Virtually no one thought it would go to $70 or $50 or even $35, though a few analysts thought it might drop to $5. This was a classic illustration of how going against the crowd can give an investor lopsided odds. The chances of oil falling to $5 and staying there were slim; many of the world's oil wells would have been shut down, money losers at that price. But the odds of doubling your money in oil shares if the price of crude merely went back to $25 were good (and, of course, crude went much higher than that).

Being a contrarian isn't easy. The best opportunities come to those with patience, courage, and a cash reserve. The opposite of going against the crowd is to get wrapped up in bidding for assets that everyone else wants. Avoid auctions, or you will suffer "the winner's curse"—the phenomenon where the high bidder usually gets a lousy deal in the end.

Negotiation:

The most effective negotiating point in any deal is when you reach "the point of indifference"—that is, when you no longer care whether you consummate the deal. In almost all markets in the world, you get the best price by giving up and walking away. Usually, the seller will chase you and come up with a lower price than you imagined possible.

"We've made a study of your money, and we've concluded
that it should belong to us."

CHAPTER 37

ZERO-SUM GAMES

The best example of a zero-sum game is Texas hold 'em poker. It is analogous to most of the derivative and hedging strategies that have sprung up in finance over the past twenty-five years.

A zero-sum game, quite simply, is a game in which for you to win, somebody has to lose, individually or collectively, the amount of your winnings (plus the casino's or dealer's charge). No wealth is created in a zero-sum game—merely passed from one player to another.

In twenty-five years of playing poker in Nevada, I won four tournaments and made the last table about ten times. One day I read a book called *Positively Fifth Street* by James McManus, which pointed out that most of the people I was playing with had drug/alcohol problems and dysfunctional family or personal situations. The book showed clearly what I'd previously suspected. In no-limit games, scam artists were often working in teams to gain an edge by communicating in code with each other. My wealth had grown to the point that sitting in a smoke-filled environment for four hours with sleazy people to win or lose $2,000 was just no longer interesting or attractive.

In the world of finance, just as in that casino, you are often playing at a disadvantage when you engage in zero-sum games. Despite this, in the past quarter century, the field of derivatives and hedging commodities has grown astronomically. When I wrote my Chartered Financial Analyst (CFA) exams from 1966 to 1969, there wasn't one page of study material devoted to derivatives or hedging. Today, it's probably half the course material. The hedging losses of mining and oil producers have run into many billions of dollars, wealth that has been transferred to banks, investment dealers, and hedge funds.

When you go up against banks with eighty-person derivative professionals who have serious mathematical training, you'd better have more than a typical corporate accounting department on your side. Hedging is a zero-sum game that has cost corporations not only enormous sums of money but, in many cases, their solvency. These practices have stolen from investors the very reason they invested in the first place—to be exposed to gold, oil, coal, or other commodity price rises. Managements and boards have unilaterally taken away the upside commodity exposure the investor sought when selecting their company for an investment.

Nothing can be built of any value by companies or countries that play zero-sum games. Casino societies meet a human need for entertainment, but at tremendous social cost. If you're going to benefit, you must own the lottery (here's a game where governments take a dollar and pay back forty cents), casino, bank, or investment dealer that runs the game. Playing these games for any purpose other than temporary amusement is just plain stupid.

"Your idea is great. Tell me about it again
when we have the next new economy."

CHAPTER 38

WHY GROWTH STOCKS ARE A POOR CHOICE FOR WEALTH CREATION

Microsoft, Coca-Cola, Wal-Mart: What do they have in common?
Two things—they are among the most recognizable and profitable companies in the world, and they have all been terrible investments in recent years.

All three were classic growth stocks in the late 1990s—companies that sold at very high price-earnings ratios, in the expectation that their profits would continue to grow. And grow they did. Microsoft and Wal-Mart are making more money today than they ever have before. They just haven't grown quickly enough to meet the market's sky-high expectations.

These companies are a good illustration of the peril of buying expensive growth stocks. Fast-growth companies inevitably slow down—and when they do, they have dramatic declines in value.

Morningstar, an investment research service, has shown how difficult it is for any business, no matter how well managed, to keep increasing its revenue and profits at very high rates for a long time. Of thousands of companies on the stock market, only a few are capable of producing an interrupted string of 20 per cent growth for a decade. For an investor they are as easy to find as a needle in a haystack.

Good Things Rarely Last: The Difficulty of Sustaining Growth

Years	Firms with consecutive 20 per cent sales growth	Per cent remaining	Firms with rising EPS	Per cent remaining	Firms with rising free cash flow	Per cent remaining
1	2,214	100	2,179	100	1,787	100
2	669	30.2	1,411	64.8	954	53.4
3	349	15.8	884	40.6	406	22.7
4	179	8.1	516	23.7	160	9.0
5	87	3.9	351	16.1	56	3.1
6	43	1.9	215	9.9	27	1.5
7	15	0.7	127	5.8	14	0.8
8	6	0.3	102	4.7	9	0.5
9	5	0.2	83	3.8	4	0.2
10	3	0.1	67	3.1	3	0.2

Data generated using the Morningstar Premium Stock Screener

In my experience, money in the stock market is made in one of two ways: by identifying commodity price trends (such as a coming shortage of oil) or by buying $2 worth of assets for $1, to give yourself a margin of safety. At Franco-Nevada, we paid just $2 million for our first set of gold royalties in the mid-1980s, on a property that was producing 44,000 ounces of gold and was right in the heart of the Carlin gold trend. At that price, we had very little downside but a lot of upside if more gold was found—and when Barrick Gold made a major discovery on the property soon after, Franco was on its way to success.

You should approach investing in the same way. Always ask how much money you will lose if things don't go as planned, and how much you stand to make if things go very well. The potential upside should outweigh the downside by a wide margin. Warren Buffett says the most important rule for making money in the stock market is not to lose. He's right. Avoid losses, and the wins will take care of themselves.

"And that's why you should trust me with all your money."

CHAPTER 39

VENTURE CAPITAL—INVESTING IN START-UPS

For fifteen years, my partners at Beutel, Goodman and I ran a venture capital fund called New Venture Equities. We concentrated on mining and oil but had representative investments in other industries. Here are some of the lessons we learned:

(A) In each five-year segment, the fund made virtually no progress for four years and then had exceptional returns in the fifth year. This reinforces the axiom that it takes at least five years to build a good business. Venture-capital investing, like entrepreneurship, is not for the impatient.

(B) Success rested on the performance of just a few of the investments. Elsewhere in this book, I've encouraged you to think of investing as a defensive game, one in which you should seek to avoid losses and put up your money only when the odds are favourable. Venture capital is the exception to this rule. You know that the majority of start-ups will fail or struggle. But that's just part of the cost of finding knockout winners.

Professional venture capitalists will often screen investments by asking themselves, "What are the odds that I can make ten times my money in this company in three to five years?" Not double their money. Not triple it. They want ten baggers. If they can get two out of ten investments to actually perform that well, then they can still get acceptable returns—even if they are wrong about the other eight.

(C) The best results came from entrepreneurial groups that had done it previously for themselves or an employer. The results from first-time entrepreneurs were dismal. Experience is a useful test when evaluating a start-up proposal. Benchmark Capital, one of Silicon Valley's most successful venture firms—it was one of the earliest investors in eBay—receives hundreds of unsolicited ideas every year from strangers. But unless the proposals come from people with some credentials, they generally go straight into the waste bucket. Not a bad policy.

(D) Investing in resource start-ups in foreign countries yielded very poor results. In venture capital, as with most serious forms of investing, it's best to stick to countries where you speak the language and understand the culture and the legal system (or lack thereof).

(E) Some people might make money in biotechnology, but my partners and I never succeeded in this area. The scientists and doctors who ran these firms tended to be extremely impractical, non-business–type people. I now avoid biotechnology investments like the plague.

"This new technology will help us keep our best
people from leaving the company."

CHAPTER 40

SETTING INCENTIVES—THE KEY TO BUILDING A COMPANY

Compensation is a large topic, one that entire books have been written on. There's a good reason: nothing is more important to running a business than good people, and very few things are more important to keeping those people than having the proper pay scheme in place. Get the incentives right, and you can create a culture of happy, motivated, and honest employees. Get them wrong, and…well, you can create Enron, where the bonus structure was sometimes used to punish those who questioned the ethics of the top executives. Here are a few valuable observations I have accumulated over a lifetime:

(A) *Deferred compensation*

The most effective program for rewarding and keeping executives was practised by an owner-operator named Pat Cleaver. In the 1970s, he ran a mid-sized, multi-industry conglomerate called Canadian Manoir. Each division manager was paid a bonus once a year, but the whole bonus was deferred for one year. If the manager earned a million-dollar bonus for 1975, he wouldn't receive the cheque until the end of 1976. If the manager left in the meantime, he forfeited the bonus. This firm had exceptionally low turnover in its executive ranks.

I've seen the same plan implemented in recent times with 50 per cent of the bonus deferred for one year. It makes a lot of sense to me.

(B) *Ten-year option vesting*

Above all, you want to make managers think about the business the way an owner would. The best way is through ownership of stock, but at my home company, Franco-Nevada, we added an option plan that vested slowly—just 10 per cent of options became exercisable per year.

If the company was successful, these options attained very large values, which, in our case, ran into many millions of dollars. But because the options vested over such a long period of time—and because the number of options an employee could get in any one year was quite small—our people tended to take a long-term view, and to stay. Our option plan covered all staff, and Franco lost something like two employees in nineteen years.

Options are reasonable tools for providing equity to wealth-creating employees. But I believe nobody who owns more than 5 per cent of a company should ever be granted this form of incentive. They should have enough motivation to act as an owner.

(C) *Profit-sharing*
The most novel plan I've ever heard of was practised by a private money management firm. The owner, whose name was on the door, retained all the equity but gave his key employees a percentage of the profits every year. If they left, they forfeited their profit share and had no residual interest in the company they had helped build. This fellow has retained his authority well into his eighties.

(D) *Communal compensation*
My base companies, Beutel Goodman & Co. (twenty-two years), Franco-Nevada (nineteen years; see Appendix ii), and BlackRock Ventures

(where I was a large shareholding director) all practised an approach of having a three- to four-person senior pool where everybody drew equal salaries. A bonus pool was also split equally. The theory was that although in some years one senior employee might create more value than the others, it would even out over time. We called this "the communal approach to executive compensation." It created true team spirit, avoided excess egotism, and cut down on morale-destroying arguments about everybody's individual contributions.

I've seen more investment dealers destroyed over compensation or bonus disputes than all other factors combined. It's surprising that more of them haven't tried some of these pay schemes.

CHAPTER 41

GOLD

I've spent the past twenty-five years involved in the gold business. As a young analyst and investment manager in the early 1970s, I visited Switzerland and found most of the money managers of that era had 10 to 15 per cent of their assets in gold or gold stocks. They believed they were simply being prudent: gold is insurance against politicians printing money, and this was a time when Western governments were printing a lot of it, running large deficits and fuelling high inflation.

It's easy to print money.

It's *not* easy to find and produce gold economically (throughout most of the past century, worldwide gold production tended to increase at just 1 to 2 per cent per year). That's why no paper currency in recorded history has ever held its value for longer than twenty-five years, and why gold is a "store of value"—an asset that, unlike cash, holds its real worth generation after generation.

To illustrate, consider an item that cost US$20 at the start of World War I. Assuming normal inflation, that same item would cost more than US$370 today. But an ounce of gold—which also sold for about US$20 in 1914—was worth more than $700 in early 2007. Through nearly a century of war, inflation, and economic progress, owning gold not only protected your purchasing power, it improved it.

But investors lost sight of gold's attributes as inflation receded in the 1980s and '90s, and fewer investors subscribed to the idea of keeping 10 per cent of their financial assets in gold. Even central bankers bought the idea that gold's day had passed. In 1970, the central banks of International Monetary Fund nations held forty-one per cent of their reserves in gold. By 1995, that proportion was down to 21 per cent, and some central banks—including Canada's—sold most of the gold they owned.

Where did they reinvest the proceeds? In US dollars, by and large, which brings us to why I am so bullish on gold today. The United States is running what I'd call a Ponzi economy, borrowing massive amounts of money to sustain its current level of consumption. It has fooled much of the world into exchanging manufactured goods and commodities for a depreciating American paper currency. The United States has even denied the foreign holders of that currency the right to exchange it for assets—recall the Unocal debacle of 2005, where the US government essentially blocked a Chinese company's bid to take over an American oil company.

Foreign countries that trade with the United States, particularly in Asia, are swimming in an ocean of dollars. America is running a trade deficit that's equal to 6 per cent of its economic output. The situation is unsustainable. As these foreign nations think twice about their currency holdings and begin to diversify them—into euros, Japanese yen, gold, or other currencies—US interest rates will have to go up, and the greenback will fall. And then gold will do what it always does when the US dollar is weak: it will rise dramatically.

This poem sums gold up well:

Gold! Gold! Gold! Gold!
Bright and yellow, hard and cold.
Spurned by the young, but hugged by the old.
To the very verge of the churchyard mould.

—*Thomas Hood, 1798–1845*

CHAPTER 42

THE POWER OF THE 20 PER CENT POSITION VERSUS HOSTILE TAKEOVERS

The great US investor Warren Buffett once said: "The greatest bargains come in buying the first 20 per cent of a public company." He would know. He made his name, and much of his fortune, by cleverly buying large minority positions in excellent businesses on the cheap—18 per cent of the *Washington Post*, 16 per cent of Moody's, 12 per cent of American Express.

Buffett's company, Berkshire Hathaway, does take over entire companies. But they are usually private firms, and Buffett sticks to a set of rules for buying them, one of which is, "We don't participate in auctions." When you try to acquire 100 per cent of a public company, you almost always trigger an auction. Xstrata, the Anglo-Swiss mining group, learned the 20 per cent principle the hard way. In 2005, it paid $2 billion—a bargain—to acquire a 19.9 per cent interest in Falconbridge, the Canadian base metals company. When it wanted to purchase the rest, Falconbridge found a friendly acquirer, or white knight, and within a year the price of the company more than doubled!

The Xstrata situation is a good illustration of the forces that are unleashed when an acquirer hunts down a public company. First, the company you're after will elevate the price by hiring investment bankers to give biased "fairness opinions" that inflate the company's true worth. You may be forced into a hostile bid (as Xstrata was), which makes it impossible to do proper due diligence. (Buffett, for one, won't do hostile bids.) The target company will expose its books and properties to a white knight. At that point, either way you've got trouble: the white knight can bid against you from a position of greater knowledge—but if he looks and doesn't bid, it means your hostile offer is too high, and you are overpaying for the acquisition.

"Government agents, sir. We're from the
Bureau of Balloon Popping."

CHAPTER 43

CORPORATE TAXES—SUCCESSFUL COMPANIES PAY THEM!

During my lifetime, I've seen numerous companies embark on complex schemes to avoid taxes. Avoiding taxes distracts management and subverts the real goal of companies: to create profits.

I have seen companies buy excess equipment at the top of the business cycle just to get enough write-offs to defer tax. I've watched them stack on mortgages or debt in rapid expansions. An entrepreneur in the cable television industry once boasted, in public, that one of his greatest accomplishments was not paying a dime in corporate income tax for nearly thirty years. He'd used billions in debt to ensure his company lost money consistently. He thought this was clever. But the long-term returns his shareholders received have been far from outstanding, particularly for a near-monopoly, and the company has gone through several episodes of financial stress.

The cable company survived, but many other tax-motivated companies don't. When the inevitable recession comes, they're out of cash (though they sure have a lot of idle production equipment that's worth ten or twenty cents for every dollar it cost). Or the business environment can change quickly. A nursing-home operator who built business through debt is hit by a new government policy that curbs medicare payments; a cable company finds itself suddenly under assault from satellite television; an acquisitive property-insurance company is stung by large underwriting losses after an unusual summer of bad weather. Before you know it, the company's ability to service its heavy debt load is at risk.

Charlie Munger one said: "In terms of business mistakes that I've seen over a long lifetime, I would say that trying to minimize taxes too much is one of the great standard causes of really dumb mistakes" (and at eighty-two, Munger has been around for enough years to witness quite a variety of blunders). This view applies to personal investments as well. Ask the people who purchased sketchy US tax shelters in the 1980s, or who bought Canadian labour-sponsored funds in the 1990s, whether the losses they suffered were worth it for the sake of a short-term tax writeoff. The last word on this topic goes to Munger: "Anytime somebody offers you a tax shelter from here on in life, my advice would be don't buy it."

"Well, here's your problem. Your house needs 128 MB more RAM."

CHAPTER 44

HOME OWNERSHIP

If you want a carefree and hassle-free life, live in a condominium or apartment. Homes are great because you are the master of your domain. The flip side is that you are also an amateur plumber, electrician, handyperson, and the employer of countless tradespeople whose common trait is rarely showing up at the appointed time. Whether old or new, a home is a series of furnace and air-conditioner problems, pest-control issues, insurance woes, cleaning problems, malfunctioning appliances, electrical and plumbing breakdowns, property tax increases, and so on, ad infinitum. People with two homes, according to a recent article, spend as much as 30 per cent of their waking hours dealing with home-related problems.

This is not to discourage you from buying a home. As long as you're prepared to put up with the headaches, I think buying a home is usually a great move and often the most important financial decision people make in their twenties. And, yes, that's still true even after the sharp increase in real estate values that's occurred in most North American cities since the late 1990s.

Higher prices make buying real estate somewhat riskier, but it's still a gamble worth taking. A home is one of the only investments with significant value beyond dollars and cents—you've got to live somewhere, and if you're not paying a mortgage, you'll be paying rent on what is probably inferior accommodation for you and your family. Homes are excellent to own during inflationary periods, especially if you've been able to lock in long-term financing at good rates (see Chapter 5). If you pay off the mortgage you remove your greatest financial burden. My parents, scarred by their experience with the Depression, declined to tie up their money in a home and paid rent their whole lives. I wish they hadn't.

Most young people today aspire to own their home, so here are a few pointers on how to approach buying one.

(1) As a starting point, approach home buying as you would any other investment—that is, look for value. Get the well-located house that needs some fixing, rather than the best house in a problem neighbourhood. Do this even if you're not the handy type: you can learn how to operate a circular saw or put up drywall. It's generally a bad idea to buy the best house on any street.

(2) Ask yourself, "If I bought this house but had to rent it to someone else, could I cover the cost of ownership—including mortgage, taxes, and maintenance—or at least come close?" You may have no desire to play landlord, but answering this question will help you avoid overpaying.

(3) Don't be afraid to walk away. In real estate transactions, as in business deals, the successful bidder of a hotly contested bidding war often falls victim to the "winner's curse." When house prices are high and rising, it's tempting for young couples to get sucked into paying more than they should, in the belief that if they don't "get into the market" right away, they'll never be able to afford a home. That kind of thinking is almost always folly. Patience is the buyer's ally here.

(4) If you think you're going to be there less than four years, think twice about buying into a strong market. In the long run, it's hard to go wrong buying a home in a place where the population is growing. But housing markets go through recessions, too—such as the one Toronto and some other major centres went through in the early-1990s, after prices had gotten out of hand.

"There must be something wrong with the new **ID** badges. They're supposed to display the value we've added to the company today."

CHAPTER 45

GOVERNANCE

Because 1 ½ to 2 per cent of US corporations misbehaved, we have a complete overreaction in the field of governance. Canadian and US business schools have rushed to create courses to train directors how to aggravate managements.

Here's a reality check. Boards of directors who meet six to twelve days a year don't run companies (or much of anything). The management that spends three hundred days and more at work has to run the show. The only real job of directors is to replace management, usually through succession, except in cases of crisis or malfeasance.

If the Securities Commission really wanted to protect the public, there are three simple rules that, if implemented, would change the system for the better:

RULE 1:

No investment dealer can ever be both a principal and agent. Banks can't make loans to companies they underwrite. Dealers can't own any shares in companies in which they raise capital.

Implementation of this rule will be resisted by the banks and investment dealers because it would cut out their most lucrative, if immoral, method of making profit at the public's expense.

RULE 2:

All multi-vote shares should have a ten-year sunset clause where they must be renewed by a majority vote of shares from all classes.

The reason multi-vote shares have not been reformed (in my opinion) lies solely with a very astute, politically connected Quebec family. This family has entrenched itself using multi-vote shares and has exerted great political influence to assure its retention.

RULE 3:

No corporate stock options of any kind can be granted to any person who owns more than 5 per cent of the shares outstanding. Other than pure greed, there is no reason an owner of more than 5 per cent of a company needs additional incentive to perform.

Owner-operators should realize they can make more from a rising stock price than from taking excessive and obscene salaries.

Governance really can be summarized quite easily by the rule of the Bible: "Do unto others as you would have them do unto you."

"The Nice Employee of the Month cut himself on the
award and is suing us for $5 million."

CHAPTER 46

THE LAW, LAWYERS, AND THE US TORT SYSTEM

Every businessperson should read *The King of Torts* **by** John Grisham. Canada's legal system has a safeguard based on the British legal system from which it is derived. That is, "loser pays." If you sue me on a frivolous matter and lose, you'll have to pay me what I spent to defend myself. The US has no such protection, and US lawyers donate billions of dollars to their political legal brethren to make sure the country never does. The US class-action (blackmail) system operates on the thesis that you will settle because it costs more to defend yourself than to settle. If you fight, you run the risk of losing your whole business to an anti-foreign jury in a backwater county court in a southern US state.

Canada's biggest funeral-home company was dispatched by a runaway jury in Mississippi.

There are one million lawyers in the United States out of a population of three hundred million people. The United States has 70 per cent of all the lawyers in the world. Its population is 5 per cent of the world's.

In the United States, the lawyers take 3 per cent of the gross national product (GNP), while all the profits of Standard & Poor's five hundred largest US companies equals 6 per cent of GNP.

I have a vivid example of the US class-action system at work. I made an investment in a large US construction contracting firm called Morrison Knudsen. The CEO had a notorious affair with a female vice-president whom he then married. While his attention was diverted, the company lost money and was sued by US class-action lawyers. Out of curiosity, to see this wonderful loss-restoration system in action, I filled out the claim forms (equivalent to tax returns) for my loss of $647,000. I then waited two years. The lawyers extracted a multimillion-dollar settlement, most of which went to them. I got a cheque for $47.

In the last great stock market meltdown, an estimated $1\frac{1}{2}$ to 2 per cent of US companies misbehaved. The result was a host of new regulations bearing the name of the two politicians who proposed them; these are the Sarbanes-Oxley Rules (also known as the SOX

Rules). For the large US company we sold our business to in 2002, these rules raised audit fees from $1.25 million to $6.5 million in two years.

My advice to Canadian entrepreneurs is that until there is real US tort reform, do not list or raise capital in the United States. Canadian, European, and Asian capital markets are large enough for virtually all capital needs. The US tort and sec red tape inflict far too high a cost for any benefits that might be received.

"And this is how we avoid spending your donations."

CHAPTER 47

THE EVOLUTION OF MY THINKING ABOUT PHILANTHROPY

Philanthropy is about giving back. You can give time, talent, or treasure (the three Ts). All are equally important. The area you support is personal and subject to various motivations including diseases suffered by individuals and their families. My passion is helping young folks get started in life through education.

In 1983 (when I was forty-three years old), I formed a foundation and set up sixteen scholarships in entrepreneurship across Canada and in Nevada. This came about because the most important $2,000 of my life came in 1963 in the form of a scholarship to McGill's brand-new MBA program. That money changed my life!

In 1995, at the age of fifty-five, I started the four-faculty benefaction project. This involves the creation of more than four hundred scholarships annually in four Canadian universities. To my knowledge, no one had ever done this type of project. I became fascinated by the subjects of goal attainment, fulfillment of life (as in, one's search for meaning) and philanthropy.

I was deeply moved by the stories of three great American philanthropists. John D. Rockefeller, Senior, was worth $200 billion in today's dollars (or about four times the net worth of Bill Gates), and he donated more than half of it to charity before he died. Andrew Carnegie, between the ages of sixty-four (when he retired) and his death at eighty-four, gave away ninety per cent of his fortune, which in today's dollars would equal $100 billion. These men lived in an age before income tax, and the fortunes they amassed dwarf the collective net worth of today's business titans. The story of philanthropist Walter Annenberg is equally stunning.

My goal was much more modest. I dedicated approximately 20 per cent of my net worth to the four-faculty project and to the foundation, which was formed to carry out many initiatives. Now Canadians only donate 44 per cent as much as Americans, on a per-capita basis. Donations ramped up five years ago, after the government extended more beneficial treatment to people who donated shares.

When I first came to Toronto in 1977, the smartest businessman I knew had lunch with my partner, Ned Goodman, and I every three to six months. (Eventually we found out he wanted to buy our company.) He had great fame and fortune. He ran unsuccessfully for political office and was a self-made first-generation immigrant. Three years after he died at age sixty-six, his family had nearly bankrupted his great business. Today nobody remembers this man!

One of my primary personal objectives is to use part of my wealth to help young people get started so they can build the wealth of our country and carry the next generation. Another objective is to create a legacy that assures I won't be forgotten. Life should have a purpose.

THE FOLLY OF ENDOWED BENEFACTIONS

Universities in the US and Canada have acquired the counterproductive habit of building up huge pools of capital called endowments. These sacred cows are the height of folly. The universities take a dollar from a donor and dole out five cents annually.

Now, there is no business in the world that runs on this type of formula. Just imagine asking a hard-nosed entrepreneur to put up $20 when a dollar of capital spending is needed. The universities go one better—they set up committees that cut the endowment payments in years where a university's incompetence produces no returns. In effect, universities say to their donors, "Look, we screwed up, so the money you put up to create scholarships for students is now in escrow until we can straighten out the mess the incompetence of our chosen money managers has created."

All my benefactions stipulate 7 to 10 per cent payouts, regardless of any capital impairment. Mr. University, you have a fundraising department. Get them off their asses to make up for any shortfalls you create in my capital account.

The foolishness of the endowment fund is magnified by a rule that says, "Ninety per cent of your money's purchasing power is eroded every thirty years." Endowment funds look great superficially but are pools of declining purchasing power. The smartest thing a university can do is issue forty-year bonds, with no repayment of principal until maturity. The institution can use the bonds to develop infrastructure that lasts fifty to sixty years, then refinance them for ten cents on the dollar when they mature.

My advice to donors and potential benefactors is: fight to keep as much of your money as possible out of endowment funds. It's often hard to avoid the tremendous mythology that envelops the university endowment fund. The efficiency with which your donation operates will be increased by the amount you can divert from these unproductive capital parasites.

HELPING YOUTH

A hundred years from now, it won't matter how much you had in the bank, what kind of car you drove or house you lived in—but the world might be a better place because you helped a young person. (For a reading list for goal attainment, a fulfilling life, and philanthropy, please see Appendix v.)

"At last! A surefire shortcut to easy money!"

CHAPTER 48

QUOTATIONS

I collect great quotations and put them up on the posts framing my office door. Here's the best gathered over a lifetime:

> Markets can remain irrational for longer than you can remain solvent.
>
> —*John Maynard Keynes*

> Faith in management is the greatest asset a company can have. Once it begins eroding, the problems begin.
>
> —*Donald Trump*

Sometimes your best investments are the ones you don't make.

—*Donald Trump*

Never do business with anyone you can't trust.

—*J.P. Morgan*

Most debt crises don't begin because somebody or some country got into too much debt, because when they were lent the money they had either the income or the asset values to justify the lending. The problem emerges when income levels fall or asset values fall and debt burdens rise relative to those.

—*Andrew Carnegie*

There is one imperative rule for men in business—no secrets from partners.

—*Andrew Carnegie*

He who makes money pleases God.

—*Muhammad*

History teaches that the time to raise capital is when it's cheap, and when you're not sure you'll need it. By the time you do need it, it may well be too late.

—*Warren Buffett*

It's only when the tide goes out that you learn who's been swimming naked.

—*Warren Buffett*

If this decision is wrong, will it be painful or fatal?

—*Matt Barrett, then chairman, Bank of Montreal*

The lawyers always take over, reducing all of life and death, passion, greed, courage, lust and glory to the desiccated vernacular of their trade.

—*Frederick Forsyth*

The First Rule of Forecasting: Give an outcome or a date, but never both!

—*management mantra*

It is not good to have zeal without knowledge, nor to be hasty and miss the way.

—*King Solomon*

I destroy my enemies when I make them my friend.

—*Abraham Lincoln*

University politics make me long for the simplicity of the Middle East.

—*Henry Kissinger*

Folks who have no vices have very few virtues.

—*Abraham Lincoln*

Don't be too smart! Don't be too tough!

—*Julius Schulich*

The best General is the one who never fights.

—*Sun Tzu*

The inevitable always happens, but not always when it's most convenient.

—*The Talmud*

A man is what he is, not what he was.

—*The Talmud*

The journey is the reward.

—*Tao saying*

"Let's not make it sound too fancy. Just say our
strategy is to make oceans of money."

CHAPER 49

SEVEN CLOSING THOUGHTS

- People who live in fear often don't live at all.

- Motherhood is a wonderful thing to behold. A self-absorbed being suddenly cares a lot more about another small human being than she does about herself.

- Business is a means to an end, namely freedom to pursue the ultimate goal of trying to make the world a better place for your having been here for a very short while.

- People only die when they're forgotten.

- Luck favours the brave.

- Don't complain, don't explain.

- The greatest thing you'll ever learn is how to love and be loved in return.

APPENDIX I

SCHULICH'S TOP TEN ALL-TIME MOVIES

1. *Gladiator*

2. *The Wild Bunch*

3. *Apocalypse Now*

4. *Carnal Knowledge*

5. *The Godfather; The Godfather, Part Two*

6. *Saving Private Ryan*

7. *The Unforgiven*

8. *Lawrence of Arabia*

9. *Bonnie and Clyde*

10. *Barry Lyndon*

THE FRANCO-NEVADA STORY—AN ILLUSTRATION OF THE LAW OF UNINTENDED CONSEQUENCES

Franco-Nevada Mining Corporation Limited started its life as a public company in 1983 by raising $2 million. Four years later, it spun off a sister company, Euro-Nevada Mining; by 1998, the pair's combined stock-market value exceeded $5 billion. These two companies, which had common management but different outside directors, formed the bulk of my wealth, and their success led me to become the benefactor of four university faculties across Canada. They also created the riches of my partner, Pierre Lassonde, who became the main benefactor of the University of Toronto's mining program with a $5 million donation in 1996.

It all started as a bit of a lark.

The origin of Franco-Nevada goes back to the early 1980s. In the previous decade, my close friend Nigel Martin and I went to Nevada two to three times a year to ski in the fabulous Lake Tahoe area and play poker. Lake Tahoe featured seventeen different ski resorts, including Squaw Valley, the site of the 1960 Winter Olympics. It is the only area with warm-weather skiing and gambling in the same locale.

During this period, I was the oil analyst and head of research at Beutel, Goodman & Company, a rising Canadian investment counselling firm. I was also the mining industry backup to the renowned and soon-to-become-legendary financier Ned Goodman, one of Beutel, Goodman's founding partners. The firm had an active merchant banking division that invested in small, early-stage companies. These projects took Goodman and me to far-off places like Costa Rica, Red Lake in northern Ontario, and Cullaton Lake in the Northwest Territories of Canada. These places featured jungles, exotic diseases, lots of bugs, and temperatures forty degrees below zero. None of the projects made any money.

An idea formed in my mind. Wouldn't it be great to at least lose money in an area that was fun to visit, while being able to write off the trips for tax purposes? I'd noticed in my Nevada excursions a lot of old mines, mills, and tailings dumps. Historically this place had produced a lot of gold and silver. The Comstock lode had financed the building of San Francisco. Goldfield and Tonopah were prolific gold and silver camps. I tried to gain Goodman's ear to form an exploration company for Nevada. But Goodman hated pure exploration in mining, and not without reason—the odds of success are long, about a thousand to one—and Nevada didn't seem to be on his list of must-do mining areas.

All this changed in 1980 when Goodman and I hired Pierre Lassonde to be an assistant mining analyst at Beutel. Pierre was a thirty-three-year-old French Canadian who had a degree in engineering and an MBA from the University of Utah. He had worked for Bechtel Engineering in Arizona and Rio Algom, a Toronto mining company. Lassonde loved Nevada too—I had found a kindred spirit! Pierre pointed out that the average cost of finding an ounce of gold in Nevada was $20, versus $50 in Canada. Now I had a fact with which to bludgeon any opponents who might try to thwart my quest for a Nevada mining toy. In 1982, $400,000 was invested to form Franco-Nevada Mining Corporation. The name derived from the fact that Pierre, the president, was French Canadian, and the exploration was in Nevada.

Well, $400,000 didn't take us very far even in 1982, so we decided to go public before going broke.

We raised $2 million by selling shares and warrants. From the start, Franco-Nevada was unique. The initial public offering was at thirty-five cents per share— exactly the same price the founders had paid for their stock when Franco-Nevada was formed one year earlier. In most mining stock deals, the promoters take stock at 1 to 10 per cent of the price the public pays later on. I had always wanted to do an "honest" mining deal where everyone paid the same price. This had never been done before, and certainly has not been done since, to the best of my knowledge. Lassonde, a young guy early in his career, was given stock options and a loan to purchase shares.

When the stock began to trade, I set about buying more shares in the open market, a very unusual thing for a company founder to do. In the world of bootlegging this is known as "drinking your own liquor." But I had a strong intuition that the company would get lucky. In the early days, I used to say: "This stock is bound for glory!"

For the next three years glory seemed far away. Led by Lassonde, Franco-Nevada participated in about forty-three Nevada and California exploration plays. Most were abandoned after drilling a hole or two. We realized that, like most junior exploration companies, if Franco-Nevada couldn't obtain a source of revenue, it was doomed.

This is where our familiarity with the energy business helped. Royalties—which allow an investor to buy a piece of the action on someone else's project— were commonplace in the oil patch. Why not try to buy some mining royalties to bring in some cash flow? In 1985, while drilling another hot prospect at Hasbrouck Mountain, near Tonopah, Nevada, I mentioned to the consulting geologist that Franco-Nevada was interested in royalty acquisitions.

The geologist, Bert Jefferies, told his partner, Ken Brooke, who spotted an ad in the Reno paper. Brooke did some checking and called to see if Franco-Nevada would pay a finder's fee. "Sure," I said, and agreed to use an old formula based on purchase price—5 per cent on the first million, 4 per cent on the second, and so on. The company selling the royalty was a junior oil outfit from Dallas that was apparently under pressure from its bankers to pay off its loans. Lassonde went to Utah and paid US$2 million for a package of royalties on 3,416 acres of ground in the heart of the Carlin Gold Trend of northern Nevada. We paid those geologists a $90,000 finder's fee for nothing more than reading that ad in the paper, but it was the best $90,000 we ever spent.

The property was producing just forty-four thousand ounces of gold per year at the time. But the land was cheap compared to anything in the oil business, and we had a theory that Newmont Mining's gold deposit to the south extended all the way up to this land. We turned out to be wrong about that, but we were fortunate anyway: in December 1986, Barrick Gold (then known as American Barrick) paid $62 million to acquire the ground covered by Franco-Nevada's royalties, then announced an increase in production to seventy-five thousand ounces of gold in its first year.

Within three months Barrick made a major new gold discovery, which was to become Goldstrike—the largest gold find in the world outside South Africa. Over the next decade, Barrick produced and developed more than forty million ounces of gold from Franco-Nevada's Goldstrike lands. Annual production rose to two million ounces per year. Our royalty package gave us an approximate 13 per cent interest in the Goldstrike complex, without having to put up any of the billions of dollars needed to build the new mines. That's the beauty of royalties. Franco-Nevada was indeed bound for glory.

Goldstrike was our first stroke of fortune in Franco. It gave us financial strength and the appetite for more properties and began Franco's transformation from an exploration play into the world's leading gold royalty company. We could not have done it without the French institutional investors who played a big role in financing our early success. Lassonde won them over with his cute Quebec French patois and encyclopaedic knowledge of gold. (He later wrote *The Gold Book*, which was published by the *Financial Post*.) Two salesmen, Jean-Yves Le Floch and Jean Louis Clement—first from Wood Gundy, later of Gordon Securities—opened doors and wallets in Paris and soon became known affectionately as "The French Connection." By the time Goldstrike hit, French institutions owned about 50 per cent of Franco's stock. They were true long-term investors. They loved Franco, royalties, and Pierre. The relationship was cemented by a memorable three-day investor tour in 1992, for which the Mirage Hotel in Las Vegas served as Franco's mining lodge.

Not all investors grasped the value of Franco's Nevada lands, however, and in 1992 we felt that the prevailing share price of $7 didn't properly reflect what Barrick was finding at Goldstrike. Lassonde and I wanted to expand the business without diluting the share value of Franco—though at one point we also considered selling the company. (Barrick, the natural buyer, was not interested—lucky for us, because selling out then would have been a huge mistake.)

The answer was to create a new company, Euro-Nevada Mining Corporation Ltd., roll all of the exploratory, non-producing assets into it, and spin it off to Franco shareholders. The two companies then embarked on an aggressive program to buy more gold royalties. By the early 1990s, Franco had acquired interests in about 36,000 acres in the Carlin trend, including Goldstrike, and Euro had interests in 43,000 acres. We branched out into oil and gas royalties in southern Saskatchewan. By the end of 1993, our tenth year as a public company, Franco had $82 million in cash reserves, no debt, and was earning $17 million in profit—and growing quickly.

Our financial conservatism was part of a straightforward strategy. Every time Franco or Euro shares went up 40 or 50 per cent, we would raise money, regardless of whether we needed it. Our view was that opportunity comes to those who can write a big cheque on short notice (see Chapter 19). A strong financial position also protects the shareholder in case of any operating problems at the mines in which we had a profit interest.

So we always kept a healthy bank account in both companies, despite our dividend policy: every year.

Franco paid out 50 per cent of its earnings to shareholders, while Euro paid a smaller, but growing, dividend. As the cash built up, we would use it to acquire large land holdings in proven gold belts in politically stable countries. We loved Nevada not only for the recreation but because mining was an important contributor to the local tax base, and state politicians understood this. We expanded by buying thousands more acres in the state, and we bought land in Australia, northern Ontario, and South Africa.

In effect, we had positioned Franco and Euro to claim a portion of the profit from development that other mining companies did in the world's prime hunting grounds for precious metals. A royalty on the growth of others is the best business to own, according to the world's most famous investor, Warren Buffett, and we had shaped our companies around that philosophy. So it was somewhat ironic that our second great windfall came not from a discovery by another mining outfit, but from one of our own.

We had never really been big believers in mining exploration—as I said earlier, the odds of success are at least a thousand to one—and had deliberately steered Franco and Euro into royalty ownership instead. The only problem was that Franco and Euro were in danger of being classified under US law as passive foreign investment companies (PFICs), which would have meant US mutual funds couldn't own Franco or Euro stock without paying penalties.

To avoid this dreaded designation, Franco and Euro jointly spent about US$500,000 to $1 million every year on five or six Nevada exploration plays. The two geologists running this program were Peter

Maciulaitis and Ken Snyder. Peter Mac, as he was known, joined us in 1984. He was a great prospector but he didn't like to sit drill rigs (spending a week on-site in the wilds of Nevada), so he brought in Snyder to help drill. Neither had much luck for ten years; Snyder, who was greatly respected, nevertheless picked up the nickname "Dry Hole Snyder." This would soon change.

In the very north end of the Carlin trend was an old gold mining camp called Midas. It had produced, on the record from 1906 to 1920, about five hundred thousand ounces of gold equivalents. (About ten ounces of silver were present for each ounce of gold.) Midas, being an old camp, had gone through perhaps thirty different landowners. Small pieces of land were picked up, drilled, and later dropped by major mining companies such as Placer Dome, Lac Minerals, Newmont Mining, and Rayrock. Nobody had been able to assemble a meaningful land position.

In the early 1990s, Franco and Euro started assembling land in the Midas camp. We really liked the location—northwest of Goldstrike between the rich Carlin belt and the Getchell gold belt, which had forty million ounces of gold in the ground. We spent about $2 million on land and, over two years, Franco and Euro put together 10,000 acres in what we called the Midas joint venture.

The plan called for the drilling of twenty holes; while drilling the sixth, in August 1994, we struck gold. We quickly expanded our holdings to 26,000 acres and kept working.

By early 1997, the deposit found at Midas had been named for Ken Snyder—who was "Dry Hole Snyder" no longer. We were constructing an $84 million mine and mill. The prospects looked excellent; we expected to be able to produce at least 250,000 ounces of gold a year at low cost. As 1998 dawned, Franco and Euro had close to $1 billion in cash, no debt, and seemed likely to produce a cash flow of $200 million a year, before taxes. On Bay Street, Lassonde and I acquired a nickname—"The Midas Brothers."

We had little experience operating a mine. My background was in investment management, remember, and while Pierre had an engineering degree, he'd been working as an analyst and running a royalty company for nearly twenty years. The legendary luck of Franco's management was about to be tested as we ventured into unfamiliar territory where our qualifications were suspect. We recognized this and hired an experienced mine builder and operator, André Douchane. He assembled a team that featured Fred Bauchrowitz, a seasoned mine manager, and David Thomas, a Wharton MBA, to ride herd on the contractor who would operate the mine.

The Ken Snyder Mine was built on time and on budget. It opened in 1999 and ran well at first. But gold prices fell precipitously to about US$250 an ounce—this was the era when many investors were chasing hot Internet and technology stocks—and the mine's production was below the levels we'd expected. It was causing great stress for me, Lassonde, and others in the company. We gave serious thought to replacing the contractor with our own team, to give ourselves better control over costs, but decided not to. Our culture had always been different than other gold-mining companies, and we didn't want to become like them.

By 2000, Franco's world was changing. We had been trying to simplify our affairs. The previous year, we'd merged Euro-Nevada into Franco to put all the assets into one public company, in the hopes of attracting investors and reducing the strain on management. Lassonde's wife had become ill with cancer and died, and we were all getting older.

Meanwhile, the royalty game was getting more difficult. Though Franco had interests in platinum, Arctic natural gas, diamonds, nickel, uranium, and copper in addition to gold and oil, we could find very few new royalties large enough to make a difference to a company of our size. We didn't want to operate mines. We could have gone down a new path of taking minority interests in individual resource companies, but we feared that would make Franco look like a complex investment-holding company.

Yet we were absolutely convinced that gold prices, which were near the lowest point in a generation, were set to rise, and we wanted to participate. We'd tried to merge with South Africa's Gold Fields, but were strung along by the country's government, which never did give approval for the deal. We abandoned the idea after eighteen months of work.

Our next move, in May 2001, was to sell the Ken Snyder Mine to Australia's Normandy Mining Ltd. In return, we got a royalty interest and a 20 per cent stake in Normandy. This put the mine in the hands of an experienced operator, freed us to concentrate on how to invest the billion dollars the company had, and gave us a large interest in the world's seventh-largest gold producer. In the 2001 annual report, Lassonde and I wrote:

Warren Buffett, the world's most famous investor, has it right when he states that wonderful bargains are available when you purchase 15% to 20% of uncontrolled companies. If entire companies are sought, a control premium must be paid. An investment done in cooperation with the management and made into the treasury of a precious minerals company can help to immediately re-rate and strengthen that company. It also allows Franco-Nevada to influence the future direction of its investment. As the Company improves and the gold industry further consolidates, *we believe such strategic equity positions in major gold producers may become very valuable.*

This turned out to be prophetic, and quickly. By the fall of 2001, Franco was still seeking a way to increase its exposure to gold, when lightning struck. Anglo-Gold of Johannesburg, South Africa, made a hostile takeover bid offer for Normandy.

We were Normandy's largest shareholder, but Anglo-Gold, incredibly, made no effort to win us over. Robert Champion de Crespigny, Normandy's chairman, was desperate to find another bidder. We approached Barrick on his behalf, but Barrick had just bought Homestake Mining, which they had recently snatched away, from Newmont's new CEO, Wayne Murdy.

We scheduled a meeting with Newmont for September 11, 2001. It was postponed when Arab terrorists struck New York and Washington. Management from Normandy, Franco, and Newmont gathered in October during the week of the Denver Gold Show, and Murdy gained a significant edge; he received about twenty-four days to conduct due diligence on his target. To buy Normandy, though, Newmont really needed Franco's cash and clean balance sheet—a three-way merger, in other words. Newmont management quickly focused on the stock-market premium it would get as the largest gold company in the world—particularly as it would be the only big one incorporated in the United States.

Anglo-Gold chairman Bobby Godsell moved belatedly to visit Franco. At that point, we hadn't yet committed to selling to Newmont. We were still open to selling our Normandy shares to Anglo-Gold, but not at the price they'd offered. After our experience with Gold Fields, we were wary of mining in South Africa, and we wanted to be compensated for the political risk. But in a four-hour meeting, Godsell never moved decisively to tie up our 20 per cent stake.

We went back to Murdy and found him to be a very tough but fair negotiator. I bonded with him very fast. He never got personal or emotional and he didn't burn any bridges. On November 14, 2001, we announced a three-way merger—Newmont, Franco-Nevada, and Normandy. It would be a few months before Anglo-Gold was finally vanquished in the fight, and the deal closed in February 2002.

Franco shareholders came out of the deal with 32 per cent of the new Newmont, the world's biggest gold company. They received a 22 per cent premium for their stock and received exchangeable shares listed on the Toronto Stock Exchange. Lassonde moved to Denver and became Newmont's president. I went on the board as Newmont's largest private shareholder, and became chairman of Newmont Capital, the company's merchant bank. Murdy proved to be a great leader, the price of gold began to climb as we'd predicted, and everyone seemed to be living happily ever after.

And the investors in our little Nevada mining toy? Someone who bought $1,000 in Franco shares when we went public in 1983 would have owned $1.25 million in Newmont shares by January 6, 2004. From the beginning to the end, it was truly a dream.

THE PEOPLE AT FRANCO-NEVADA AND EURO-NEVADA

Craig Haase and his wife, Charlotte Haase. This team was the outside counsel to Franco in the first seven years of its life and joined the company full-time in 1990. Craig is one of Nevada's leading mining lawyers and is unique because he also holds a degree in geology. He built and managed Franco/Euro's key Nevada operation. In Canada, legal work was conducted for more than a decade by the very able Sharon Dowdall of Smith Lyons.

Andre Douchane is a mining engineer with more than twenty-five years of experience. We brought him in to build the Ken Snyder Mine at Midas.

Ron Binns—my longtime chief financial officer is a real gem.

David Harquail, Al Hamilton, Steve Aaker, and *Geoff Waterman*—a team of two geologists, an engineer, and an accountant. They provided screening and support in virtually every acquisition in mining and oil.

Ann Brown ran our Toronto office, and has more than twenty years of service acting as my assistant.

Donna Yoshimatsu—our manager of Shareholder Relations and Pierre Lassonde's assistant for more than a decade.

APPENDIX III

SEYMOUR SCHULICH'S LIST OF OIL COMPANY WEALTH BUILDERS

1960s   – Ranger Oil
         – Murphy Oil
         – Inland Chemical

1970s   – Puma Petroleum
         – Pennant–Puma Oils Ltd.
         – Trinity Resources Ltd.
         – Canadian Bonanza Petroleum Ltd.
         – Bonanza International

1980s   – Canada Northwest Land
         – Canadian Merrill
         – Campbell Resources

1990s   –   Franco-Nevada Mining Corporation Ltd.
         –   Peyto Petroleum

2000s   –   BlackRock Ventures Inc.
         –   Canadian Oil Sands Trust

A TRIP TO THE ARAB WORLD—APRIL 2006

THE SCORPION'S TALE

A wild camel was about to ford a river when a scorpion approached and asked for a ride to the other bank. The camel said, "How do I know you won't sting me?" The scorpion replied, "If I did that, we would both drown." The camel thought it over and said, "Okay, hop on my back."

As they crossed the river, the scorpion stung him and the camel became paralyzed and started his fatal plunge below the flowing waters. In his last gasp, he asked the scorpion, "Why did you do such a suicidal thing?" The scorpion replied, "This is the Middle East!"

I flew to Dubai on Emirates Airline, the tenth largest in the world. The airline has US$37 billion of aircraft on order. No other air carrier's order book comes close. Middle East oil exporters will take in some $320 billion US this year. It's estimated these funds finance 45 per cent of the US current account deficit.

The plane featured a cubicle (for first class) which could be turned into a completely horizontal bed with a foam mattress and blankets. More than five hundred movies and compact discs were available, plus gourmet meals at any time the passenger desired. (In other words, this airline was the opposite of Air Canada.) The thirteen-hour trip equalled my experience six years ago with Singapore Airlines.

THE FIRST STOP: UNITED ARAB EMIRATES (UAE)

Population 2.4 million plus 2.3 million guest workers
GDP per capita US$23,000

The population is deceptive, as there are 2.3 million non-citizens from India (a two-and-a-half-hour plane ride away), Pakistan, Burma, and Uzbekistan.

The expats are there on renewable contracts. (I met a driver who had been there for twenty-two years.) Their children, born in the UAE, are not UAE

citizens. Any expats not working or caught commit-
ting a crime can be immediately deported to their
country of origin. No unemployment insurance or
welfare exists. The UAE thus has only dedicated, hard-
working immigrants who want to be there. They have
a public health system with long waits and poor service. The lowest workers (taxi drivers, guides) all carry
health insurance and go to private clinics (a lot of the
clinics are run by British firms).

There are six keys to understanding the UAE:

1. Seven sheiks formed the union in 1971 and are
    benevolent dictators. There's no parliament or
    democracy. They have a strong police/army com-
    posed of very tough Yemeni mercenaries. There's
    virtually no crime. The UAE is like Singapore in this
    regard.

2. Wages for immigrant guest workers run US$200
    per month for construction and US$400 for taxi
    drivers.
       Guest construction workers are housed ten to a
    room. They have fixed-term contracts, no unions,
    and no way to return home early, as the UAE keeps
    their passports. They are slaves with a term limit.
    Newfoundland's seals have more rights.

3. After 9/11, the Arabs, mainly Saudis (Saudi Arabia is a two-hour drive), pulled most of their money out of the US, fearing bank account freezes. Money has poured into the UAE, funding a Ponzi-like building boom. Many houses, apartments, and pieces of land have turned over five to six times since 9/11.

4. The sheiks, in total, have four official and up to forty-six unofficial wives. The wives do hit the malls, spas, and beauty salons, and are pretty westernized under their black robes. There are a mere forty-two shopping malls in Dubai to service 1.2 million people. We never ran into any native citizens working. Their children are being educated in England and Europe. Most contractors are British. The malls we saw were as good as or better than those operating in Canada. English is spoken everywhere and is on all the signs.

5. The oil in the UAE will run out in seven years. The real estate explosion is their answer to what comes next. Almost all the developments are on palm-shaped peninsulas fanning out into the shallow Gulf waters. Global warming could put them all underwater in fifty years. Meanwhile, it's good to flip real estate in a booming market.

6. The clergy in the UAE appears, like in Quebec, to be on the decline. There are forty television channels of junk; there is Internet Wi-Fi everywhere; liquor is freely available; and there are no beggars, litter, or graffiti anywhere. Singapore, look out: the UAE is following and exceeding your formula.

DUBAI (POPULATION 1.2 MILLION; CONSTRUCTION MANIA)

- US$90 billion in projects were under construction in 2006, utilizing 15 per cent of all the tower cranes in the world.

- The tallest building on the planet, the Burj Dubai Tower, is under construction and due to open in 2008. It will be twice as high as the Empire State Building in New York.

- The world's biggest ski dome is in the 5.2-million-square-foot Mall of the Emirates.

- The largest theme park in the world is due to open in 2009. It's called Dubai Land. It will feature life-size dinosaurs.

- Huge real estate developments, called Palms, are being created from dredged ocean material in the shallow offshore area around Dubai. A series of private islands in the shape of the world's continents is also being created; they can only be accessed by helicopter or boat.

In five years Dubai will be attracting more tourists than Orlando and Walt Disney World.

THE BURJ AL ARAB

I stayed at the Burj Al Arab in Dubai. It's a seven-star hotel. Yes, it really is worth the rating! The modest two-level, three-thousand-square-foot hotel room (they're all this size) costs US$1,500 per day and is absolutely beyond description. There are three butlers and a floor manager for every twelve suites. There's staff everywhere (twelve at the front entrance alone). There's gold plating everywhere.

The health club covered an entire floor (the eighteenth) and was the best I have ever seen. It would take several pages to describe it.

The twenty-seven-storey hotel sits on an island about two hundred yards offshore and took twenty-nine months to build. The gold plating is overwhelming, as are the mosaics, marble work, fountains, overall decoration, furnishing, and restaurants.

The Burj Al Arab must be seen to be believed. It is unique and surpasses any other hotel I have ever seen.

IS DUBAI THE COMING FINANCIAL CENTRE OF THE MIDDLE EAST?

Oil reserves are running out fast and only contribute 7 per cent to GDP. Dubai has found a niche recycling the oil wealth of its neighbours. It's also building business parks and investing in cyber technology, shipping, and transport terminals. The city has launched a Gold and Commodities Exchange. Wall Street firms such as Morgan Stanley are opening their first Middle Eastern offices in Dubai. HSBC has recently set up shop there.

The Gold Souk (market) has three hundred stores. Dubai historically has been a wholesaler of gold, and smuggled gold to India. I went on a tour given by the World Gold Council, which maintains a large, very competent operation in Dubai.

Huge amounts of natural gas are consumed in the UAE by water desalination plants and power generation. This consumption will cut into the source from neighbouring Qatar's exportable surpluses in the years ahead.

Steel prices in the UAE are up 40 per cent, and labour costs recently rose as much as 30 per cent from a very low base. Inflation is starting to be a huge problem in the UAE and will get much worse before it abates.

Perhaps the most amusing aspect of my three days in Dubai was the visit to the 1,200-foot-long indoor ski hill, built inside the second-largest shopping mall in the world. (The Mall of the Emirates is 6.5 million square feet; only the South China Mall—at 7.1 million square feet—is larger.)

The Swiss built the ski facility, which manufactures snow at night and has a fully operational 1,200-foot quad-chair lift. The facility supplies all ski clothes and equipment for a two-hour session. It's 27°F inside. I wanted to try it out but it was fully booked for days.

OMAN

The annual per capita GNP of Oman is US$13,400.* Sixty per cent of this derives from 770,000 barrels per day of oil production; the country has oil reserves of 6

* Compare to Saudi Arabia at US$12,000 per person, with a population of 22 million.

billion barrels. Gas reserves are 7.5 trillion cubic feet, and gas is produced at 15 billion cubic feet per day. Half the gas runs the country's power and water desalination plants; the other half is exported as liquefied natural gas (LNG).

Oman has government medicare, which oil pays for. The pediatrician is the obvious king of the doctor set. Half the population is younger than twenty. Having multiple wives is the obvious way to solve the pension-fund crisis and create lots of support for the geriatric set.

If you're looking for the ultimate contrarian country investment, Oman could be it.

SALALAH, OMAN

Salalah is a modern, fast-growing city with a tropical atmosphere, the second-largest city in Oman, and has a population of three hundred thousand. The total population of Oman is 2.5 million. The country is what the UAE must have resembled thirty-five years ago.

US$90 billion is roaring into the UAE, but virtually nothing is going to Oman. It's austere, tradition-bound, has a dry climate except at monsoon time, and is very hot. (Temperatures go up to 122°F.) Our guide wore a black burka, which must have been wonderful in the cloudless 96°F heat. She was in her early twenties and had twenty-six brothers and sisters, who derived from one father and four women. It must be funny loading this group into the family suv for a holiday in the northern open desert. With a family this large, it's interesting to reflect on things like dinnertime, bathroom access (I couldn't get in with only one older sister), and choosing television channels. Moreover, remembering your kids' names in this cultural set-up could be challenging.

EGYPT

My first impression of this country of seventy-two million people was filling out a form that asked about the model of camera, every unit of currency, and every piece of jewelry and each watch I would carry ashore. Every tour bus had an armed guard (who slept 90 per cent of the time) and three police car escorts (very comforting for the wives). The last country in which I had seen this type of protection was Indonesia.

Per capita, GNP annually is US$4,400. (Canada's is $33,000 and the GNP of the United States is $42,000.)

The tour bus convoy started at Safaga, a small port on the Red Sea, and proceeded 180 miles to Luxor.

We passed through a moon-like desert for half the distance then entered the Nile Valley. This 70- to 90-mile swath of land is interlaced with irrigation canals and is the breadbasket of Egypt. Produce includes wheat, sugar cane, cotton, plus an array of fruits and vegetables.

The route had fifteen to twenty military checkpoints. Nobody moves about too freely way down in Egypt land.

We visited the Valley of the Kings, a major burial ground for the pharaohs and families who lived in Egypt three to five thousand years ago. These complex tunnels and chambers are highly decorated with hieroglyphs and quite worth the visit.

The valley is an armed camp where I spotted at least twenty two-man guard posts featuring soldiers with Kalishnikov assault rifles. The visitors have returned after the killings six years ago of twenty-four European tourists. Luxor and the whole Nile Valley are third world, with pockets of three- to four-star hotels on the Nile. There are lots of idle river-tour boats at Luxor.

We proceeded to a mind-bending set of ancient buildings, statues, and sculptures at a large compound at Luxor. The three-square-mile Karnak complex was close, but we missed it due to time and security constraints.

Our return trip at night allowed us to see the mosques lining the Nile River Valley. Their spires are lit up with various coloured neon bulbs. The Aswan Dam, 240 miles away, provides electric light for roads, houses, and mosques. At no time as I crossed the 75-mile swath of the Nile Valley were there less than five mosque towers visible in all their neon-lit glory. It's pretty obvious religion is crushing this land. Our guide said life priorities were religion and family. (Religion ranks ahead of family!)

Our convoy left fifty minutes late. The guide explained: *"Inshalla"* ("It's God's will"). Every screw-up in Egypt (and there's no end of screw-ups) is explained away as *Inshalla*.

The country has four regions: northern, southern, Numidian, and western desert. Fifty-five per cent of Egyptians are farmers, and 50 per cent are illiterate. The Nevada desert is a tropical garden compared to the Egyptian desert.

In rural Egypt men have up to four wives. Gold is money here. All dowries are paid in gold or camels (no paper, thank you).

Our armed Egyptian bus marshal slept like a baby the entire three-hour trip back from Luxor to Safaga. Want to cure insomnia? Join the Egyptian bus marshals.

ALEXANDRIA (THE PORT OF CAIRO, POPULATION 8 MILLION) AND CAIRO (POPULATION 20 MILLION)

The trip to Alexandria went via the Suez Canal, which is about 101 miles long and 984 feet wide. It carries 14 per cent of the world's ocean-trade traffic. Our 68,000-ton vessel paid a toll of US$375,000 to go through the canal.

Cairo, the noisy, polluted, crowded capital of Egypt, featured traffic congestion of epic proportions fuelled by low gasoline prices—twenty cents per litre. Another prominent feature was the unfinished house. Everywhere in Egypt I saw houses with columns sticking out of the roof, protruding rebars splayed upward. It's as if people were adding one more storey to the house or apartment building, but ran out of money. Our guide explained the phenomenon. It's simple— you don't pay tax until the building is completed. This flawed taxation policy has created a country of ugly unfinished housing. There are not a lot of clothes dryers or central air conditioning. The plumbing in many cases runs down outside walls.

It's important to understand that Egypt is a country that's 90 per cent desert!

There are few signs in English anywhere in Cairo. Ninety per cent of Egyptians are Sunni Muslims, and 10 per cent are Coptic Christians.

The pyramids are impressive, but the vendors surrounding them make tourists run a gauntlet of harassment second to none I've seen elsewhere. The people could use a dose of the discipline I saw in China.

There was more military presence around Cairo than any other city I have visited. The Hilton was surrounded by troops, hiding behind mobile steel panels and sporting vests capable of stopping a grenade. All visitors, tourists, and people who want to eat lunch in the hotel undergo an airport-type check-in. Again, there was a sleeping bus marshal on each vehicle plus police car escorts.

The amount of bureaucratic red tape in Egypt looks stifling. People travelling must pass checkpoints everywhere. In short: if Egypt were a stock, I would short sell it.

Two days after I left, terrorists exploded a bomb in an Egyptian resort, killing ten people and wounding sixty.

REY, THE BUSBOY—A GLOBALIZATION STORY

More than 200 out of a crew of 650 on our cruise ship were Filipino. They work eight to ten months non-stop for about US$250 per month. They are fleeing a country with unemployment at more than 50 per cent and average wages of US$120 per month.

Our twenty-five-year-old busboy, Rey, has a mechanical engineering degree and is the only wage earner in his six-member family. He will return to finish the required year of apprenticeship upon completion of his contract with the American Cruise Line, which operated a top-rated ship.

As I cruised with passengers, 90 per cent Americans, 5 per cent Canadians, in the lap of opulence and five-star luxury, we couldn't help but wonder if in fifty years, the passengers would be Chinese and the crew largely American kids.

A READING LIST FOR GOAL ATTAINMENT, A FULFILLING LIFE, AND PHILANTHROPY

BUSINESS BASICS

Influence – The Power of Persuasion, by Robert B. Cialdini (Recommended by Charlie Munger; more than a hundred given away; a must for marketers, or for those who wish to understand people. If you read only one of the suggestions on this list, this is the one.)

The Tipping Point, by Malcolm Gladwell

How To Win Friends and Influence People, by Dale Carnegie

Blink—The Power of Thinking Without Thinking, by Malcolm Gladwell

Made To Stick, by Chip Heath and Dan Heath

A FULFILLING LIFE

The Paradox of Success, by John R. O'Neil
(Success often lacks fulfillment.)
What Happy People Know, by Dan Baker
(The only real thing you can control is your own behaviour.)
Man's Search for Meaning, by Viktor Frankl
Rules for Aging, by Roger Rosenblatt
(Ideal for folks over sixty.)
Don't Sweat the Small Stuff, by Richard Carlson
Myths, Lies, and Downright Stupidity, by John Stossel

PHILANTHROPY

Titan: The Life of John D. Rockefeller, Sr., by Ron Chernow
(Rockefeller was worth $200 billion in today's dollars; he donated 50 per cent of it.)
Carnegie, by Peter Krass
(Carnegie was worth $100 billion in today's dollars, or twice what Bill Gates is worth. Between the ages of sixty-four and eighty-four, he gave 90 per cent of his fortune away.)
Legacy: A Biography of Moses and Walter Annenberg, by Christopher Ogden

ACKNOWLEDGEMENTS

I would like to honour many of the important people who formed the bedrock upon which a life of philanthropy and business success was constructed. Folks such as business partners who, covered by anecdotes in the book, will not be mentioned again here.

At least one-third of the wisdom in this book is derived from my father, Julius. He was a dress designer and small businessman who prospered before most of the textile manufacturing migrated to Asia. He fought in World War I in the Royal Canadian Field Artillery. No one could have had a better father. I dedicate this book to him.

I derived lots of wisdom and early support from my mother, Bessie, and my dear older sister, Edith, who provides an excellent sounding board right up to the present.

My wife of thirty-eight years, Tanna, who was raised in Halifax, has been a great credit to my family. Her listening skills make her beloved by all. (In life, people like listeners far more than talkers.) She taught me one of life's great lessons, that self-praise is no honour. Tanna raised our two daughters, Debbie and Judy, in whom we both take enormous pride.

The daughters (through their marriages) brought me the sons I never had. Both Simon Serruya and David Stein are probably far superior to any natural sons I could have sired. They are both very talented entrepreneurs and mensches. They are helping produce the only true wealth anybody ever leaves in their life, wonderful and beloved grandchildren.

Ann Brown, my assistant, has been dedicated to me for twenty-nine years. She is a jack of all trades, a gatekeeper, and a wonderful person with whom to have shared office life. Ann supplies a lot of the empathy I need to navigate in today's world.

Donna Andrejek handled the typing of the manuscript as changes were incorporated. She was a terrific help on this project.

Lawrence (Larry) Bloomberg, a best friend for forty-three years—which is something, as he still looks about sixteen—has been an invaluable sounding board. He is the ultimate connector and fundraiser. (I obtained a ten-year immunity for this testimonial.) His serious demeanor is nicely offset by his wife, Fran, who has a smile for his every frown and has become a Forest Hill doyenne of great stature.

Derek DeCloet aided in the writing of this book by adding material to many of the chapters. At thirty-four years of age, he has the perspective of youth, which he adds to a book aimed at young adults. All this was accomplished while he continued to produce regular columns for the *Globe and Mail*'s Report on Business.

The name for this book was suggested by Lorraine Luba. I am indebted to this charming mother of three and grandmother of five children. Lorraine is the wife of Bob Luba, a regular walking companion, a former CEO, and a very astute businessman who continues to provide counsel on many Canadian boards. I've had the privilege of knowing him since 1985. He served with distinction on the Franco-Nevada board for many years. In retrospect, maybe we should have had Lorraine on our board, as well.

The story behind the cartoons shows how the Internet has changed the world. My daughter Debbie gave me a desk calendar featuring the work of about ten cartoonists. I selected two and looked them up on the Internet. I contacted Ted Goff in Kansas City, who had an inventory of 1,800 cartoons. I sent him the draft of the book via email. He found two or three cartoons for each of the chapters. I then convened a committee of four people, whose average age was thirty and who had read the draft. By majority vote, they selected one cartoon for each chapter. This whole process took two weeks. In my youth, without the Internet, a project such as this would have consumed six to eight months. Viva the Internet! I'm grateful to Ted for his work.

Canada's leading entertainment lawyer, Michael Levine, provided guidance and found a publisher, which is not easy when you consider that publishers receive approximately four thousand manuscripts a year. Through this process I met Jordan Fenn, the vice-president and publisher of Key Porter Books. He gave me wonderful insight into his industry, and his enthusiasm to drive the marketing efforts is greatly appreciated. Jonathan Schmidt, Key Porter's experienced managing editor, gave wise counsel in putting the final touches on the book.

INDEX